'My Name Is
Len Davies
I'm A Football Scout'

By Peter Shelton / Len Davies

With a Foreword by Francis Lee

Published - Shelton / Davies

First Published 2000

Shelton / Davies
120 Normoss Road
Normoss. Blackpool. FY3 8QP
Lancashire.

© Peter Shelton

ISBN: 1 85314 207 7

Cover and Book design by Peter Shelton
Printed in Great Britain by:
Biddles Ltd.Woodbridge Park Estate
Woodbridge Road
Guildford, Surrey. GU1 1DA

Joe Royle and Len Davies

"Joe and Len at Platt Lane Training Ground"

Contents

Page No.

Chapters...

This Book is dedicated
To my Lily…

Len Davies

My Name Is Len Davis - I'm A Football Scout

I would like to think that in nearly fifty years in my part-time career as a Football Scout that I have never willfully hurt anyone in any way in my endeavours to succeed in my duties. As I reminisce the years gone by, extremely enjoyable years, I hope that the publishing of this Biography, will give all my friends and aquaintances some of the pleasures I gained from my experiences.

This is my first attempt at trying to communicate by means of the written word. It is neither my Profession, nor my vocation, but I would hasten to add, in my determination to succeed, that I am neither sick nor impudent, hence my perseverance. My reasoning is from a passionate, sincere and honest motivation to bring you, the reader a distinct vision of unobscured, but simple realistic facts of Football. Facts gained from almost fifty years of Football Scouting and its associations. I have no desire, or intent, to offend in my reminiscences. Nor do I seek to conform with the Establishment (The F.A. etc.), the media or the experts. I may express opinions, which differ, and I hope, lend themselves open to discussion at many levels. The objective of the book, whilst termed a 'Biography', is to convey to the reader, observations and minor deviations from the game. It will, hopefully, lead to a glimpse into my personage and character, these glimpses, often humorous, but nonetheless, factual.

Having met and rubbed shoulders with many people over the years has made me a much richer person, not financially perhaps, but rich in friendships made. Friendships with the likes of 'Big' Charlie Fletcher

(Sheffield Wednesday Scout) and John Shore (West Bromwich Albion Scout), without these, I'd be a lot poorer in memories. Characters like these as your friends could never have a value placed on them. Sheffield Wednesday and West Bromwich Albion would certainly wish they had Scouts of the fibre of these men today.

I owe thanks to many people in various areas and none more so than Peter Shelton, my friend and Scouting associate during his time at Manchester City, for cajoling me and 'bullying' me to start and get the book finished. He then had the arduous task of reading through my many files and creating a semblance of order and presenting it to you.

My thanks go to the many schoolteacher associates who over the past years, have worked so hard in providing 'Little Jimmy and Johnny' with a game of Football, and all the help given to me in my endeavours, unsung heroes all of them.

To my group of Associate Scouts who work alongside me - Joe Yates - Hassan Sultan - Ronnie Jamieson and Peter Booth. They are a great bunch of lads whom I trust implicitly to do a good job. They are a part of the Footballing fraternity - all pals.

But most of all I want to dedicate this book to my long suffering wife, Lily, who for the past 55 years has put up with this bad tempered and often-volatile character I bless her patience. She has been my best find to date.

To a group of Angels (Sisters and Nurses) at Tameside Hospital, Ashton-Under-Lynne, who nursed over me when I was in a sad state of health, thus enabling me to recover and finalise this book. No words of mine can qualify their wonderful work.

I hope you all can enjoy an hour or so of reading.

Len Davis

It has taken a lot of time, preparation, and a great deal of research on Len's and my part to complete this venture. It is with a lot of gratitude, that we would like to thank all the people listed below, for their time and patience and, in some cases, a lot of tolerance in making this venture possible.

Francis Lee	Ex - Player & Chairman Of Manchester City
Alan Ball	Ex-Manager of Manchester City
John Maddocks	Manchester City Club Historian
Simon Marland	Bolton Wanderers Club Historian
John McClellan	Leeds United Club Historian
Dave Thomas/Fay Walter	Manchester Evening News
Mark Wiley	Manchester United Club Historian
Lily Davies	A kind lady with a lot of patience
Len Davies	For putting up with me
Ron & Pat Gregson	Kind and generous Support
John Nicholson	Manchester Sports Ltd, Friend and kind supporter

Peter Shelton

Foreword_____

By **Francis Lee**
Former Chairman of Manchester City &
Ex-Manchester City and England Player

Football Scouts are an integral part of any successful Football Club with an ongoing Youth Policy. Without them, the steady flow of young hopefuls would not be available to the Progressive minded Clubs. They obviously need a constant supply of the right kind of young talent, to be developed, into the right kind of player required for the modern game. That's where the Scout comes in, searching out and finding these talented youngsters as early as possible. Finding them early, in order to teach them, the techniques that have been overlooked in years gone by.

The influx of foreign players shows us, that on the continent, technique is very important. The game in the early days, late 50's, 60's and 70's, developed the type of players that had plenty of skill, courage and conviction, apart from a spell in the 80's and early 90's, where the game resorted to the 'Long Ball Tactic'. It is from this period we started to fall behind the technical skills of the Continentals.

The new Soccer Academies, now being set up by the progressive minded Clubs, will eventually bring these talented youngsters through to the professional ranks, with the skills required to compete at the highest level and with the necessary technical skills. In the fifties, Football Clubs attracted players the best way that they could. The bigger and more successful a club, the easier it would be to attract the better players. There were no Soccer Academies in the early days, you acquired your skills at School and playing as often as you could. I would sometimes play twice a day if necessary. Most Schools in the fifties played Football and Scouts could monitor the progress of any boy at an early age that showed any kind of ability or skill.

Today it is very different, a lot of Schools don't provide organised sport at all. At present date, in and around Manchester, there are some two hundred Schools that don't provide any kind of sporting activity, so where would the youngster at these Schools, develop his Footballing talents? That's why we at Manchester City set up the Satellite Centres around the Manchester area. Manchester City knew they could attract a lot of possibles and hopefully turn them into the most likely prospects, they also increased the Scouting Staff to meet the demands of finding these young hopefuls.

The modern Academies today, not only provide a Footballing Education, but an Academic Education too!. Upon reaching the age of sixteen and if your Footballing skills are of the required standard, then instead of the YTS Schemes that were offered in the past, you can now be offered a Scholarship. The likely prospect will now get an Education where he will at least have to try to get some kind of degree. Something to fall back on in the event that he doesn't succeed as a Footballer.

When I first became Chairman of Manchester City, we made a lot of changes. We developed Maine Road and our Platt Lane Complex. We built a Training Facility that any Parent would be delighted to bring their youngsters to, to learn and develop their soccer skills. In the first year I worked alongside Paul Power in helping him set up the initial stages of the Academy. The Academy is something that is very close to my heart and always will be. The Academy is Manchester City's future.

The good young talent coming through will be its lifeblood.

Len Davies has been a part of Manchester City in that respect. He has brought in a lot of fine Football Players over the years that have gone on to serve City well. Even today in the 'Twilight' of his Scouting career, he is still involved in spotting talented youngsters. Young talents like, Lee Crooks and Terry Dunfield from Canada. Terry came to Manchester City for trials when he was about thirteen. Ted McDougal the ex-Manchester United player recommended him along with some other boys, also from Canada. I asked Len to look at these boys and inform me if there were any worth taking on, he recommended only Terry. He was then asked to monitor the boys progress and to maintain a contact with his parents and what a great job he did. Terry and his parents were convinced that Manchester City was the place to develop his soccer career.

Today Terry is a part of City's Youth set-up and making good progress through the ranks. He has a great attitude for such a young man. Anyone, who will give up his life in Canada to come over here to play football, well that's commitment. I feel that if Len hadn't put the time and dedication into looking after this boy, he wouldn't be here today.

Len Davies has been a great contributor to Manchester City and his efforts for the Club, and the players he has brought here, will always be remembered.

Francis Lee

Introduction

The Football Scout   " Is he, really necessary? "

Like anyone in life today, we all dream of being successful in whatever vocation we may choose, but whatever we choose, we must have the ability to be able to perform to a high standard in order to achieve our goal. Some of us are naturally gifted and go on to achieve our goal without much of a struggle. There are those of us that have the ability, but lack the knowledge to use it to our best advantage, but with an insatiable desire to succeed and, given the opportunity and, with a little help, our dream might come true.

Being born with a God given talent and having the opportunity to be able to display this talent is something most people dream of. But having this talent and **not** having the opportunity to be able to use it is unthinkable. It would be a perfect World if we all could have this opportunity, but what would we have left to dream about. We all need a 'Goal' to aim at. Not everyone will make it, but having the opportunity to try, is far better than having had none.

In order to survive we all need to make a living in one way or another, like, driving a Bus or digging ditches. Some people prefer to rob Banks. Whatever way you choose to make a living, what better way than doing something you enjoy, like playing football. It's every young boy's dream when growing up to be able to emulate his favourite soccer player, going into thunderous tackles like Roy Keane or David Batty.

Making that 50-yard pass like David Beckham into space for his fullback to make that overlapping run, but dreaming won't get you the opportunity. It's getting a game of Football, and being seen by the right people displaying your talents, that will make your dream come true. Not everyone will make it; it's having the opportunity to try, which is important. This is where the Football Scout comes in. Looking for the youngster playing for his School Team or his Sunday League Side. Showing that little something special, that catches the Scout's eye and ending up with him being offered a trial to show what he really can do. Being accepted at a higher level and the chance, with the right kind of coaching, to improve his soccer skills.

Let's take a look at ten-year old 'Billy Smith'. His dream has finally come true. He's been selected for the first time, to play for his School Team. He arrives at the place of Combat, the School Playing Fields. He enters the changing rooms a little nervous and apprehensive, but excited at the prospect of getting out there on the pitch to do battle against his deadly rivals. The games Master starts to pick his team. Billy is, by now, really excited at the opportunity he is going to have of getting the ball on the halfway line and dribbling past five opponents and hitting an unstoppable shot into the top corner of the net. The crowd cheering wildly, going on to play for England and scoring a 'hat-trick' at Wembley in the Final of The World Cup.
…"Smith you will be in Goal because your, the tallest"
…"But Sir! I'm a striker"
…"And I'm the Teacher, you will go in Goal"

At School the Games Lesson lacks the characteristics you might associate with a lesson. In my experience, the games lesson taken by the Teacher is often only a case of organising a bunch of kid's for a game of Football, picking two Captains and asking them to select their teams. Then the Teacher takes an active part in the Lesson by becoming the match official. Imposing his whims and fancies on the game as he sees it. Offering very little constructive criticism on how the lesson is progressing e.g. 'Get Stuck In', rather than explaining why he should have made a tackle in that instance.

The 'Junior League's' have basically the same problems with teams being run by the man next door because he has a big car, and can get 6 kids in it, and 22 sets of parents doing the coaching from the sidelines. These are only 'basic general comments' and not necessarily intended to misdemean the efforts of these people who, are very often, extremely dedicated and work very hard to provide youngsters with a game of Football. My comments will, I hope, show why I think it is important that the 'Talented Players' get the opportunity to be able to develop their God given skills and improve the Natural Progression of the State of The Art game of Football.

There are exceptions to the rule of course - In some Schools and the 'Junior Leagues' you will often find the dedicated lover of this grand game of ours who has gone to the trouble of getting qualifications in 'Coaching', or the 'Ex-Pro' helping out. This is the beginning of the players Education in the 'Art of Playing Football'.
'A Natural Progression'.

...Let's take the same ten year old Billy Smith playing for his Sunday League Team in the local Park on a freezing cold day in February. Running around with all the confidence of youth trying to emulate the skills of his favourite player and dreaming of one day being able to play for his favourite Team in the F.A. Cup Final at Wembley. All red-blooded Football fanatics have had that dream, but only a small minority ever gets the opportunity, the 'Special Players' with the natural skills. This is where dreams are made. Getting a game of Football and being seen by the right people and being offered the chance of 'Natural Progression'. Trials for a Professional Football Club, acceptance, coaching, progress from Youth to Senior Football.

'Enter the Football Scout'

In the Beginning God created the Earth. He took six days we are told and on the seventh he had a rest, but what you were never told is that he didn't really rest. He created the 'Football Scout'. Football Scout's come in all shapes and sizes. There are Mum's and Dad's - The Postman - The Milkman - The man who works at British Aerospace and the decrepit old man with the dodgy 'Ticker'. Anyone can be a Scout as long as he or she has the desire to see that this beautiful game of ours is played properly with all the natural skill's God gave us. The Football Scout was created just for this purpose, to find the special player, with the necessary skills required to make a Footballer.

"Where does he find these special player's?
And how does he decide,
That they're special?"

Finding them isn't the problem, go to any open space with grass on it and you should find a bunch of kid's playing Football. These are potential soccer players ranging from the age of six and upwards. Most of them can play Football, but it's the special ones with the natural skill's that the Football Scout is looking for?

"How do we spot the special ones?
What, is the Scout looking for?"

Most Mum and Dad Scouts think their offspring is that special one.
"Our Jimmy can dribble and pass a ball better than Ryan Giggs".
They may be right.

"So how do we go about sorting the specials from the 'Bunch of Kid's' playing 'Football',
On the open space covered in grass.
What is the something special?
That the 'Football Scout' is looking for?"

Every Scout has his own opinion of what makes a special player e.g. Good Dribbler - Good Tackler - Good with his Head and a shot like a 'Speeding Bullet'. The special one must have a combination of these plus a strong desire to succeed. Some of them can dribble like Ryan Giggs or Maradonna, some can tackle like Tony Adams or Roy Keane, and some can pass a ball like David Beckham, but to find one with all of these skills is extremely rare indeed. That's why we have - Good Defenders - Good Mid-Field Ball-Winners / Ball Players - Good Attackers. Each special player has his own brand of skill that will be developed by the Coaches once the 'Football Scout' has found him.

I've been a Football Scout ever since I was ten years old, ever since my Grandad took me to Maine Road on September 20th 1947 to watch 'City v United'. 78.000 people were packed into the ground to watch an exciting 0-0 draw and on the way home my Grandad kept saying to me.

> "That City centre forward will never make a Football Player as long as he lives. He can't control the ball. If he can't control it how's he going to score?"

Control that's the first thing you should look for in a player - Can he control the ball - Whats his first touch like. Without possession of the ball and possession is the 'Prime Factor', you're never going to score.

There's no special training to become a Football Scout, just a warm coat, a pair of wellies and, an insatiable love of the game for the many cold and wet winter days you will spend looking for that 'Special Player'. The one who will catch your eye with that extra special bit of skill his God given talent allows him, that one day, may afford him the opportunity to develop his skills at a Professional level.

Football has changed drastically since I was a boy in Manchester 50 years ago. When we played with a tennis ball in the Street, or in the School Play-Ground with my mates with our old battered leather 'casey' as we called it, that held so much water when it got wet, it was nigh on impossible to kick. Now, along with better diets and training and medical treatments that keep todays players in top-class condition - the new lighter plastic coated Footballs - the Footwear and lightweight Clothing, the game has speeded up to break-neck pace. Regardless, of the pace of today's game, and the different tactics being imposed on the modern day players, the Football Scout's job is still basically the same as before. The endless visits to the local Parks looking for the youngster that has that little bit of skill that sets him apart from the others.

Go to any Park, on any given weekend and you will see half-a-dozen potential football players ranging in age from nine to sixteen trying the clever tricks of their favourite player, dribbling past two defenders, and thumping an unstoppable shot into the back of the net. Or the Winger leaving the full back for dead, getting to the bye-line and making a pinpoint cross for his centre forward to nod past the despairing goalkeeper.

When you find what you think is the right player, you then must judge him over two or three games against differing types of opposition to see if there is some kind of consistency in his play. Occasionally after one look, you may be convinced you've found the right one, but only occasionally. Once you find that special someone you think has the potential, he will then, hopefully, be given the chance to go through all the coaching and training. Then, depending on his progress, to the time when he will be given the opportunity, to show what he can do in a match situation. If he is successful he will go on to gain an apprenticeship and hopefully on to Senior Football and a successful and worthwhile career. Not all will make it, there will be lots of disappointments, but there will also be lots of successes.
"How do we know we've found the right one?"
We don't. We all think we've found the best prospect, beyond that, it's out of our control, it's up to the individual to work hard on the skills he has to maintain that consistency that will eventually lead to him achieving his ultimate 'goal'.

A successful career in Football

Without the Football Scout little 'Billy Smith' might never have the opportunity to fulfill his dreams and wouldn't that be a travesty of injustice. Whether he makes it or not is irrelevant. It's having the opportunity that counts. I started scouting for Manchester City in 1993 and so far I haven't found the best player in the world yet, but I have given a lot of youngsters the opportunity to start off on the road to doing so, one day one of them might prove me right. I haven't spotted that special someone yet, but I know someone who has and it's about him that this book is about. His name is Len Davies.

I met him on my first day as a Scout down at Manchester City's training ground at Platt Lane Manchester on a freezing cold day in December 1993. City was holding trials for under-14 prospects. I stood alongside him and watched as the games progressed. I was having great difficulty in determining which were the good players from the average, they all looked good to me such was the standard on view. There were some good young prospects out there that day. Nicky and Anthony Fenton, Jeff Whiteley, Lee Crooks and Gary Mason. They've all gone on to sign professional contracts with City.

Len was making little notes about the various players and writing down little comments about what he liked in their play. I was totally confused, the standard was well above anything I had previously been connected with, and I'd been involved with Junior Soccer for some eighteen years, but not at this level.

I listened intently, because I thought I would definitely learn something here today.

"He's got a nice first touch"
"I like his aggression, he wants the ball"
"A good turn of speed, did you see him pull away from the fullback?" he said to me as he made his notes.
At the end of a very good mornings football, and all the parents and prospects had left, Terry Farrell and Jack Chapman, City's Youth Development Officers and all the other Scouts that were present, met in one of the changing rooms to discuss who we thought were worth taking on.

I didn't have much input at this juncture. I just listened and occasionally agreed with what was said. At the end of it all, the majority of boys that were agreed by all to be the best prospects, Len had circled their names on his sheet. I thought that I could learn something here and I certainly have since. I've had many good conversations with him up to the present day and his help and guidance has been invaluable. I would now like to introduce you to him and in his own words tell you about himself and his belief that...

'The **FOOTBALL SCOUT**' is really necessary.

Peter Shelton

Chapter 1

"A Matter of Opinion!"

I became a Football Scout at the young age of thirty-three. The main reason for this was, that I wanted to be involved with the game that I loved, in whatever capacity I could. I really wanted to be a Football Player, but as I will explain in Chapter 2, I just didn't have what was required to make the grade. I had the desire and the attitude; I even had, although I'm blowing my own trumpet, a fair amount of skill. Unfortunately, because of someone's opinion, I wasn't accepted, that's Football.

Opinions! Football's full of them, right or wrong, decisions are made because of them.
"I think 'Billy Smith' is the best crosser of a ball I've ever seen!" might be one opinion.
"I think 'Billy Smith' lacks pace and has a poor attitude, but he crosses a great ball" might be another.
Someone will ultimately decide that because he lacks pace and has a poor attitude, he isn't worth taking a chance on. Then again, because he is the best crosser of a ball than anyone has ever seen, that he is worth taking a chance on, his other problems can probably be adjusted. That's what Scouting is all about, forming an opinion and making a judgment and hoping that your recommendation will be accepted and on the way to becoming a Professional Footballer.

All the top clubs in the U.K., upto present date, have realised that investing in the recruitment of better Scouts, is a sound and sensible way to fight the constantly escalating costs of running a successful club and maintaining a good top-class professional squad. The current market value of purchasing an established top professional is from £2 to £10 million pounds and in some cases, even more, but by recruiting good capable Scouts and setting up a much wider Scouting network, the progress of the local youth can look a much better proposition.

One or two of the top clubs are now beginning to reap the rewards of the last five to ten years of investing in their Youth Development Schemes. For example, at Manchester United there's Beckham, Scholes, the Neville brothers and Nicky Butt etc.etc. At Leeds United who, at this point in time, have a crop of homegrown youngsters displaying their talents in the Premiership. 'Jonathon Woodgate and Paul Robinson' joined Leeds as twelve-year olds, discovered by local scout Eddie Beaglehole. 'Harry Kewell' came to Leeds via Australia at fifteen, he came over on a scholarship. 'Alan Smith', another homegrown product of the Leeds scouting networks, he also joined as a twelve-year-old. 'Paul Kelly, Ian Harte and Stephen McPhail' joined Leeds as fifteen year olds, products of Leeds Irish Scouting fraternity. A sound investment, if I may say so. Even at Manchester City, who having battled their way back into the First Division, are beginning to show the fruits of their investment in Youth Development with their fine facility at Platt Lane Manchester and a good crop of youngsters that are beginning to make the breakthrough, namely...

'Leon Mike' - A strong bustling type of centre forward in the Alan Shearer mold - Holds the ball up well, good in the air and an excellent finisher. Not made the first team yet, but not far away.

'Shaun Wright-Phillips' - Is the son of Ian Wright of Arsenal, and now occupying a place in the Burnley line-up. Shaun is a talented prospect and highly thought of by Manchester City. I was tempted to say a 'chip off the old block', but Shaun is a different type of player to his famous father, as anyone who has seen him play will agree. He made the first team, albeit temporarily at the end of 1999. If he has a flaw in his make up, it is his slight build, but he has the attitude and skills that will take him to reach the same dizzy heights gained by his father. He will do it his way and not by being compared to his famous Dad and what he's achieved.

'Steve Hodgson' - England Schoolboy International and currently playing Youth and Reserve Team Football at City. Very highly rated by Goalkeeping coach Alex Stepney.

'Terry Dunfield' - From Vancouver, Canada. Currently in the England Youth set-up, and one for the future.

'Jeff Whiteley' - Northern Ireland International at seventeen and doing well in the first team.

'Gary Mason' - Did well for the first team 1999/2000 season - Scottish U-19 duties also.

All of these are down to good Scouting and investment in Youth Development. A good Scouting policy is essential in order to compete for the young talent that is out there. Good Scouts must essentially be devoted Football people, people capable of assessing the needs required and the persuasive powers to convince the likely prospect that the club the Scout represents, is where he will get the best opportunity to become a professional Football player.

The Scout is an integral part of any successful Football club and should be recognised as such. In the past, little recognition, by Clubs, Directors and some Managers, has been given to the Scout, the little man with the 'Flat Cap and Scarf', who devotes all his spare time in ensuring a regular supply of prospects. I believe that in the not too distant future, people will want to know how or where did 'Billy Smith' come from? The Scout is an invaluable necessity. I must admit, that Scouting recognition has improved somewhat over the years, but there is and should be, room for improvement. In my opinion, very little consideration is given to the amount of time that is spent scouting. You can't put a valuation on the time you spend. The meagre rewards should be made more attractive in order to recruit good Football judges, genuine Football men.

It may not seem significant to some Club Directors and Management Teams, but the subscribers and supporters of Football clubs are very much interested in the clubs achievements of bringing young players through, as it would seem to them, all the achievements in recruiting talent are down to Managerial intellect. This isn't always the case. In many instances, it is down to the persistence, and belief of the experienced Scout, that has helped the club procure the services of a boy who eventually makes the grade. It hurts any decent Scout to see a boy turned down and then later make the grade elsewhere. This will always happen in this 'funny old game', but in many cases a good Scout will be determined in that he, in his opinion, will not detract from his beliefs. He creates his own standards and stands by his beliefs and opinions. A little pat on the back and a thank you now and again wouldn't go amiss.

Initially, Scouting begins with a Football enthusiast, who desires to continue with his interest in the game, possibly after retiring from playing as an amateur or Pro'. In the beginning, as a stopgap 'filling in time' hobby, but eventually it grows on you and begins absorbing you. You make a few notes and do a brief report; it keeps on growing on you. You now feel you're qualified to express your own opinions, you're learning to Scout, you're becoming more and more involved and want to do more than just fill in a team sheet and write out a report. You wish to express the progress some youngster is making. You feel that he could measure up to the standard of the boys at the club for whom you are scouting. You're now ready to take it to the next level.

You will now venture to approach the Manager or coach for the boys details and to find out if he is free, to take a trial with your Club. If given the OK, you may then talk to the boy and his parents. You can be very lucky and meet both Mum and Dad! This is a bonus indeed, unfortunately, as we approach the millennium, we meet so many boys whose parents decide to separate and you then have to placate both parents, sometimes a delicate situation. You're learning further, now it's diplomacy and you realise, that additional to your ability to spot a potential star, you have to earn the respect of the boy and his parents. Your handling of these situations can often secure the signature of a prospect by virtue of winning over Mum, Dad or both. Once you have acquired the boy's signature, you can then pass on any relevant family domestic issues to the Welfare Officer, as we are fortunate enough to have at Manchester City. You still wish to be a top class Football Scout? Then never be afraid to listen and learn from others experiences.

I became a Scout for the reason I stated. You may fancy the idea of becoming a Scout for whatever reason. If so, then maybe I can offer a little advice and my 'opinion', on what is required. I think perhaps, without presuming too much, that my forty-five years experience, as a Scout should entitle me to express, what I feel is needed in order to accomplish this.

TIME... Essentially, you will need a lot of this. Time is a factor that is a must in order to become a good proficient Scout. If a likely prospect needs viewing, you must find the time to go and look and not.
"I'm too busy today, I'll go and look at him next week".
That's too late, another Scout has just 'nipped' in and obtained his signature. A good Scout will make the time.
ORGANISATION... You need to be a good organiser and have the ability to be ready in your objective. Simple little things that are so important, silly as they may sound, having a notebook and a pen at all times. They won't make you the best Scout in the World, but you will find that they are extremely necessary.

PREPARATION... Don't leave anything to chance. Always make sure, when setting off on an excursion to scout a likely prospect that the game is on. The weather may be bad and the game has been called off. The venue may have been changed on the night before. Establish contact with the Club concerned if need be - the Kick-Off time may have been changed. Being prepared at all times is essential. These are just the basic requirements of becoming a good Scout - Having plenty of Time, being a good Organiser and being prepared for any eventuality.

Now! How do we set about our objective? I always try to arrive at the game I'm going to view as early as possible in order to set out my plan of attack. You may be meeting the parents of a possible prospect - or to make contact with the team managers to get their list of players, team colours - or any other information that is pertinent to you.

Once you have established contact, never be conceited or overbearing in you initial approach. Be polite and always have your Club I.D. with you. Be forthright if questioned and be as honest as is possible. Don't lie or, if you will pardon my expression - 'Bullshit'. Your initial contact can be the first of many you will make with this particular person, or persons. If you don't have an answer to a particular question say so, and that you will endeavour to find out the answer for them. Try to establish your parameters - you are trying to establish your character - people who lie, are soon found out.

Most established Scouts, like myself have built a good reputation and a lot of us within the game, though often, competing for the talents on view, have a respect for each other. Most of the established Scouts, say in and around the Manchester area, often engage in friendly conversations and with the odd bit of humour 'chucked' in. A good example of this was on one occasion when I went to Woodbank Park to watch Stockport Boys v Manchester Boys. It was on a beautiful morning in April. I was still at Leeds at the time, and I, along with some other Scouts, Billy Fenlon - Manchester City, Harry Baron - Crystal Palace, Joe Schofield - Bolton Wanderers and a lad from Oldham, who's name escapes me, were all stood along the touch-line preparing to watch the game.

We had all parked our cars in the car park that was about half a mile away from the ground. All of us, barring Billy Fenlon, had left our topcoats and raincoats in our cars. We stood along the touch-line listening to Harry Baron, who was a lovable 'pain-in-the-proverbial', telling us about all the prospects he had found, when Billy Fenlon asked me a question, which was very well timed, because it had just started to rain as they were about to Kick-Off.

> "Len! Who is, without doubt, the most intelligent Scout amongst us?"
> "You are Billy!" I replied.

Harry Baron almost burst a blood vessel, followed by a convulsion. He then began rhyming off a list of talent that he'd found, over the thirty years he had been a Scout. He then urged, in his indignation, as to why...

> "Billy is the most intelligent Scout?"

I said...

> "Because he was the only one with enough sense to wear a 'Bloody Raincoat".

Sorry if I digressed a little. Now back to the Scouting.

After viewing the game and you have finally made your way home, it is now time, to transfer the information you have gathered, from your notebook to your match report. Write a report firstly for yourself containing your views on the game. I initially did just the junior scene, when I first started, and I prided myself on putting together my honest opinions of...

(a) The game.

(b) The conditions.

(c) Any unusual occurrences / problems etc.

(d) Best talents on view.

(e) And finally, any recommendations I might have, or players, I might need to have a second look at.

I always made copies of my reports; you never know when you might require some reference at a later date.

You will notice, how we are now talking about accumulating information, this is a prime factor. Getting information on the particular age groups you are covering and the proposed areas to cover. Gathering information from the Local Leagues, by contacting the League Secretaries and obtaining League handbooks. You may find that in the area you want to cover that there may be 4/5/6 different Leagues with age groups ranging from Under-9 to Under-16. Each age group may have anywhere from, ten to twelve teams in each age group.

You are now beginning to build up a picture and reference of what is required. Start building up your local knowledge, there is never enough information you can accumulate. Listening to local gossip and picking up on whats happening in the Junior Leagues can be most helpful. Someone else's opinion is fine, but always try to separate their opinions from the true facts by making your own judgment and checking out the gossip.

Initially, I would concentrate on the younger age groups say, Under-9/10/11/12 and 13. Then when you feel you are beginning to establish yourself and are feeling confident in spotting one or two likely prospects. You will then want to try your 'eye' at the Town Team Schoolboy level at Under-14/15 in your particular area. The more proficient you become, the more you will then want to move on up etc. etc. Whilst you are concentrating on the Schoolboy scene, it is most important to establish a good working relationship with the Schoolteachers responsible for Football in those particular areas. I am extremely grateful for the help I have had over the years and for this, I offer my gracious thanks to all of them.

After awhile you will become progressively aware of your involvement as you absorb the steady progress of your early prodigy. Watching as he climbs the rungs of the ladder to a possible apprenticeship and, you sincerely hope, on to the day when the Club informs you that they are signing him to a Pro' contract. You have now become established. In some cases, you will receive a bonus for this.

Not all Clubs have a Scouts Incentive Scheme, but if you are fortunate enough to Scout for one that does, well, it's a nice 'bonus'. Scouting is mostly voluntary and vast riches for Scouting are not available, most Clubs offer expenses and such like. In most cases, It is reward enough in itself, in knowing that you have given some youngster an opportunity to make a career for himself.

Bonus schemes were none existent in the early days. Now they are commonplace amongst the top-flight clubs. No such schemes were available at Manchester City until Peter Reid arrived and introduced them in 1992. I, a little naively, accepted my role as a Scout at City on a 'gentleman's handshake', in that I would enjoy the same terms that I had under Don Revie at Leeds United before coming to City. It was at Leeds, when a Scouts prospect that was signed to a Schoolboy Form, the Scout would receive £100. When the same boy signed an apprenticeship agreement, a further bonus of £100-£200 would be forthcoming. If he went on to sign a Pro' contract, another bonus would also be due.

I received two bonus's each, whilst at Leeds, for two Manchester lad's, Gary Felix and Robert Skilling. I also received a bonus for them signing Pro' contracts;

they didn't quite reach the standard required to break into the first team, and were released when they were 18/19 years of age. This was prior to Don Revie taking the England Managers job and me deciding to join Manchester City. As I mentioned earlier, I accepted my role at City on a 'gentleman's handshake', that I would enjoy the same terms as those at Leeds United. Unfortunately, no such scheme was in place.

I approached Mr. Chris Muir, who was the Director in charge of Junior Football at that time, about my early signings of Dave Bennett and Ray Ranson and my assumption of receiving my gratis bonus. I received a friendly pat on the back and a well done and an assurance that the matter would be looked at, but I received nothing. I was given an interest free loan of some £400 to purchase a decent second hand car, repayable to the Club over twelve months. Again, naively, I went along with this. I procured the signatures of numerous other boys namely - Clive Wilson - Steve Kinsey - Geoff Lomax - Earl Barratt to name but a few, but no bonus's came my way, only a pat on the back and a well done. So I was overjoyed when Peter Reid set up the bonus scheme for Scouts similar to that I'd had with Leeds. Jimmy Frizzell, who was Chief Scout at City at that time, up dated this in 1994. He set up a scheme where we would receive £500 for a prospect signing Pro' and a further £1000 if he played five first team games. I was unlucky with Lee Crooks as he signed Pro' before the Peter Reid agreement of 1992. If one of your players, who signed on after the 1994 agreement, went on to play ten full International games, a bonus of £5000 would be forth coming.
Scouts joining a club today, under a new updated scheme 1998/9 agreement, will receive a contract signed

by the Scout and the Club complying with whatever terms are agreed upon. If you are only part time, then it will be expenses only. If these schemes were available when I took up my Scouting duties, I would be a rich man today. I believe my twenty-seven years at Manchester City have been rewarding to the club and, pity is, as I draw my days to a conclusion that I should be trying to ensure that my fellow colleagues in Scouting are treated with more respect, than they have been. These are the men, who go out to find tomorrow's stars.

It is an enjoyable pastime, but I feel the money that is now in the game, rewards of a higher nature should be more forthcoming. The P.F.A. and Club Directors and management, should be getting together and offer acknowledgment to a body of men who do a wonderful job too cheaply. The odd ticket or two to watch a home Match, is scant reward for all those long winter hours spent searching for new talent. I'll say this about Don Revie, God Bless his soul, he would listen to your pleas and succumb to most requests. If he were running this club today, he would say...
"Let them have a piece of the cake too".
As you progress you will accumulate a list of people who you will value as friends. Those who you feel you can place a trust in. These kinds of associates are invaluable. Those who will be very helpful, and those who will help you on the odd occasion. You may find people willing to help, but only for their own benefit. Being honest and earning your respect are vitally important.

I can recall on one occasion whilst I was with Leeds United. Don Revie asked me to cover a game involving Burnley. He asked me to have a look at the winger named Dave Thomas, who went on to play for

Everton and England. I actually went twice to look at him, but I was disappointed on both occasions. My report on him made this obvious. It contained no 'Bull-Shit', just my honest opinion, that I didn't think he measured up to Don's lad's, at that time of, Giles, Bremner and Lorimer etc.etc. Dons valuation of £400.000 / £500.000 was a lot higher than mine was. My opinion, was an honest one, it was what I thought. The Media and others at the Club thought differently. I asked Don if he wanted my honest opinion or what the others said.
He said no to Dave Thomas and to me he said...
"Len! Always say what you think".

If you want to be a Scout, you will need to be honest, not only to those you work with, but to yourself too. Have confidence in your judgments and hope that the opinions of others do also. There is a tremendous feeling in knowing that your opinions are right when you see your prodigy out there, with the crowds cheering him on to scoring the winning goal, or making a great ball-winning tackle in an important game for his club, a great feeling indeed...

"And that's just, My Opinion! ".

Chapter 2

"The Early Days"

I think I had better introduce myself and tell you a little about me before we continue with the Scouting bit. My name is Len Davies I'm a Football Scout and I work for Manchester City Football Club. I've been here since 1974, and prior to joining City, I was at Leeds United, but I began my Scouting career at Bolton Wanderers in 1954.

I was born in Droylsden near Manchester in 1922 and I had two loving parents. My father was Welsh and my mother an Irish Catholic. A perfect pairing, one might think, for what was their favourite hobby, fighting. They didn't hate each other; they just loved a good old-fashioned verbal argument and the occasional punch up when they had had a 'little drink'. It often took me, and my three brothers, one sister and stepsister, all we could to keep them apart once they started. I don't want to paint the wrong picture; everything in the Davies household wasn't all doom and gloom.

Times were hard in the 20's and 30's and money wasn't plentiful, my father worked full time and very hard at his job in the Cotton Mill, but he made sure that we were all well fed and provided for. We were brought up in a disciplined manor and taught the meaning of respect and the difference between right and wrong. If we ventured from the right path, we were well punished and never strayed a second time, but it was a happy household besides being a well disciplined one. I was a fairly good scholar, and was always in the top six of my class. I think that I also acquired from my dad, good penmanship and a sharp brain. I had lots of hobbies and interests like, music, books and the Theatre, but for as long as I can remember my main interest has always been in Football. In my later years I have learnt, that the passing of time does not mean that I am obliged to lose interest in what is my favourite sport because I can no longer take an active part in it. It has now become my favourite hobby, Scouting.

I got married on April 29th 1944 to my Lily, we've been together for 55 years, and have raised three children. Brian my eldest, who is 53 years old and married to Janet, emigrated to Australia 25 years ago. They now live in Sydney; they have a grown up family of Gary 28, Graham 26 and Maria 21. Brian is a fan of City of days gone by and a big fan of the late great Dave Ewing.

My second eldest, Lesley is 44 years old and married to Joy; they have a son Simon and a daughter Tracey. Simon is 22 years old and is about to embark on a career in Teaching and Tracey works for a Finance Company.

My youngest is my daughter Jean 42 years old, is married to Ronnie Deakin a local Bricklayer and character. They have a daughter Lisa, a wild and unruly 18 year old, very much in the modern idiom, hard to control, but loveable nonetheless. Jack, their son is 7 years old and has retired from Football, temporarily that is, to become a Boxer. He enjoys his regular visits to Hattersley Boxing Club to watch his Idol, Richard Hatton our local light-welter weight Champion. Richard spent a season at Manchester City with our U-11 Squad, I found him playing for Glossop Juniors about ten years ago. He could quite easily have followed his Father and Grandfather into the Professional Football game, but I think his real skill is in the Boxing Ring.

Like so many schoolboys who develop a measure of skill at the game, I had dreams of making the grade to professional Football and basking in the limelight and applause of the cheering crowd. My early dreams began to be fulfilled when I was selected for the Ashton-Under-Lyne Town Schools XI at under-14 level the year was 1936. Later that same year I was invited for trials for the Lancashire Boys Team, this really was an honour and I thought I was on my way to becoming a professional Footballer. I went for my trial at the same time as another local lad, Harry Johnston. Harry was eventually selected and went on to sign for Blackpool upon his leaving School. Harry played his entire career for Blackpool, and won a few England caps too. My dreams were short lived however, because although I was proficient enough, my physique and smallish stature was against me being offered the chance to play at a higher level. I accept this now, but it was difficult to accept at the time being so young and full of dreams.

There was another youngster at the same School as me called Mick Ormerod. Mick was a classy left-half back with brilliant skills, but somehow never succeeded to make it like Harry. Mick was captain of our School team Moorside. Mick had no real parental support, no one to push him. His father was a Mill worker and a widower with family responsibilities. Harry went to Fairfield School. Harry's father, was in the Haulage Trade, quite prosperous and ever attentive. I think what evaded Mick was that little element we often mention called 'luck'. He should have made it, I've no doubt about that and I still feel the same some 60 years on. Mick joined the Army in 1939-1945, and never came back to football as far as I know, and the right people didn't observe him, like many others from that era.

Scouting at that time was still in its infancy and many good players were lost, or overlooked because of this. Organised Football for the younger element, 9-13 year olds only really excisted at School. Sunday Club sides were non-entities until around 1945. This was initially frowned upon, by all that governed Football. The Sunday Observance Society was against any sport being played on the Sabbath. Parks Football pitches and Athletic Grounds were considered out of bounds for quite some time. There was an overall feeling amongst a great many people, that a right to play Football on a Sunday should be given. Finally the Government succumbed to pressure and permission was finally given, this was around 1950, but it wasn't without its problems.

Sunday Football in the initial stages was mainly open age Football and not for the younger element. An outlaw body established itself and became known as the Sunday Football Association. The Football Association failed to recognise them and severe restrictions and sanctions were imposed on all Clubs and Officials who participated or played in this illegal Football. I actually played for the Gorton Sunday League, which was a member of this 'Villainous and Rebel Organisation', that operated illegally until the early fifties.

Pressures exerted by the F.A. made it impossible for them to continue as a pirate body, even though they were well organised. We played, from 1946/7 onwards in a Nationwide Sunday Cup. Referees were banned from officiating and all decent playing facilities were placed out of bounds. Eventually all who participated in the outlawed Sunday Football, relinquished to the pressure imposed by the F.A. and raised the 'White Flag' of surrender and joined the F.A. or their respective County Associations. From then onwards Sunday Football prospered and we saw the emergence of Junior

Football becoming established in the Fifties. This also started to interest the Pro-Clubs - 1st/2nd/3rd and 4th Divisions and some of the better Non-League Pro-Sides. Some useful players were picked up from the better-organised Sunday Teams.

As I grew older I continued to play as an amateur at differing levels from 1936 to 1955. I played in the Lancashire Combination League - The Cheshire League - Southern League and the Kent League. I also played in numerous Combined Services matches during my stint in the Armed Forces in the Middle East with the Royal Engineers. It seems rather funny to me now, that although I was never offered the chance to play at the professional level when I was a young lad, I was offered the chance to have a trial for Aston Villa whilst playing for the Army.

An Officer in our regiment, other than doing his Army service, was also a Scout for the Villa. I was playing for the Army versus a Benghazi XI at the Bengahzi Stadium in 1949. I was playing at wing-half and had a very good game, and after the match he offered me the opportunity to have trials for Aston Villa. When he asked me my age and I told him I was 27 years old, well that was that. I continued playing in the amateur ranks until I was 34 then I decided enough was enough with my true ambition never realised. After being demobbed from the Royal Engineers and at the end of my playing days, I began to ponder on what the future might hold for me in my favourite pastime of Football. I loved my Football and I had no regrets at not making it in the pro-ranks, but I still wanted to be involved in the game in some capacity. That was partially answered in 1952 by a group of lads who played for West Gorton F.C.

They were a side playing in the South Manchester & Wythenshawe Saturday Amateur League. They asked me if I would be interested in becoming their Secretary and Manager. I agreed and was duly appointed as a General 'Do-It-All'- Manager - Secretary - Provider of and Kit cleaner - Find some cash organiser - Put up the Nets and anything else you care to name. I didn't mind this, because they were a great bunch of lads ranging in age from 18-25 years. They were mostly lads who had just completed their 2-year National Service and were still reasonably fit and a good Footballing side to boot. They came from all walks of life - Engineers - Draftsmen - Tradesmen of all description. Our Goalkeeper was Daily Herald Photographer Roy Young, and he was more than capable.

We developed into quite a good side and we earned praise from every side we came up against in a League that was of a very good standard. The Scouting network that watched this League quite frequently picked up the late great Roger Byrne the Manchester United full back. We had a few players that went for trials with Blackpool / Liverpool / Bolton and Wolves. None I'm sorry to say ever made the grade, but were at least offered the chance. In particular, Len Cross, a solid Centre-Half - Vinny Docherty and Fred Stanley, very hard working defenders and Eric Murtagh, left wing. I'm convinced they would have made the grade if given the opportunity of good coaching and training. It also goes to show that even at their ages 18-25, the Scouting fraternity, were prepared to come and look and offer opportunities. Whilst I was involved in my role with West Gorton F.C. I took the opportunity to aquire my Referees Badge and so I took up the whistle and became one of the dreaded men in black.

I began to referee in Manchester's Gorton and District League. The standard was very good and demanding, but I found the challenge to be both interesting and stimulating. It was probably, without doubt, the hardest league in the Northwest. I enjoyed this and it kept my interest in football very much alive. However, the West Gorton F.C. side began to fall away in standard as some of the boys got older, and began to pack up playing. Eventually the team folded.

Refereeing kept my involvement in Football alive, but it wasn't enough, so I began to look for some other way to pacify my craving for more involvement. Whilst refereeing I found that I could also do a little Scouting so I wrote off to both Manchester clubs offering my services but! "Sorry No Vacancy" was the reply. I then wrote to Bill Ridding who was the Manager of Bolton Wanderers.

Bill was one of the old-school Secretary-Managers of that era. He started his career playing for Tranmere Rovers and then after a brief spell at both Manchester City and United in 1929-33, he came to Bolton, but cartilage problems forced him into early retirement. He rejoined Bolton in 1950 and was appointed Manager at the same time as he was appointed as Trainer to the England Team for the World Cup in Brazil. He went on to manage Bolton for seventeen years, the second longest serving League manager next to Matt Busby. Sadly, Bill passed away in September 1981; he was seventy years old.

Bill passed on my letter to George Taylor who was Chief Scout. George was one of the games real gentlemen and a lifelong 'Trotter' fan. George had been at Bolton all his soccer life and rarely did you ever see him lose his temper and never did he swear at any time to me or in the presence of anyone, which was quite remarkable.

Football is a very frustrating game at times, and colourful language has been known to be used, upon more than the odd occasion. I've been known to utter the odd 'expletive' or two in my time, but that doesn't mean I'm different from anyone else, working on the shop floor of a factory for all the years I did, meant my language was as colourful as the next mans. George invited me down to the training ground on a Thursday night for a chat and it turned out that we had a lot in common regarding our Football. We both played for Ashton Boys Under-14's, he some 10 years earlier than me of course, but it gave us a starting point in our association. He went on to obtain an apprenticeship and also made it into the Pro-Ranks, I wasn't so fortunate.

I was finally off in 1954, on a life times adventure as a 'Football Scout'. I learned a lot from George in the beginning regarding Scouting, he also taught me something I didn't know much about then, but became invaluable to me later on, Tolerance. George asked to go one Saturday afternoon to Whaley Bridge from my home in Gorton Manchester on a miserable rainy January day to have a look at a young centre forward. It poured down throughout the entire game. I had, unfortunately, left my umbrella on the Bus en-route to the game. I was literally soaked to the skin and I naturally had a good moan to George when I made my report on the lad. He started laughing because he had had to fly to Scotland on the Friday to view a lad up there. It snowed from the moment he arrived and he never saw a ball kicked and was stranded there until the Monday because of all the flights being cancelled due to the weather. The weather is only one of the hazards of Scouting; it's something you just have to live with. Frustration was another hazard I had to cope with in my early days as a Scout for Bolton.

When making approaches for talented schoolboys to invite for trials, the more glamourous clubs like Manchester United and Arsenal etc. would be a more tempting proposition to them and made your job that little bit harder. This only spurred me on to work even harder.

My duties in the beginning were to concentrate mainly on the Manchester areas and to look at the Under-14 Town Team Schoolboy games and the Saturday afternoon Youth Club Leagues. The first boy I recommended was called David Farrar. I first spotted David playing at Under-13 for his School, Nicholls High School in Ardwick Manchester. I invited the lad to come and have a look at Bolton and from there I was asked as to how I rated him because he was unknown by any of the other Bolton Scouts. I said that I thought he would make the Manchester Boys Trials and also the Town Team and possibly the Lancashire Squad. Frank Pickford the top Scout at Bolton then followed up, my recommendation, and he confirmed everything I had said. David and his mother, who was a single parent at the time, were invited to Bolton to meet with Manager Bill Ridding.

I accompanied them both one Sunday morning in the close season to meet him. David and his mother were overjoyed when Bill Ridding invited David to join Bolton Wanderers upon finishing his education. Mrs. Farrar asked Bill Ridding if it would be acceptable to them if David were allowed to learn a trade as a precaution should he fail to make the grade as a Footballer. This presented no problem to Bolton, as the Gerrard Family, who were a Firm of Builders Merchants, were on the Board of Directors at Bolton, this would allow David the opportunity of serving an apprenticeship in Joinery along with his Football training, an acceptable agreement to both parties.

Mrs.Farrar unknowingly allowed David to sign forms with Bolton and they were put in Mr.Riddings safe until David became 14 years old or upon leaving School the following season whichever would be correct. They would then be registered formally, as would be the correct procedure, but signing before the boys fourteenth birthday was against F.A. Rules.

David continued to progress with his Football and did make the Manchester Boys Town Team as I had predicted and he was soon awarded his first Cap for England Schoolboys at Wembley. Bolton continued to show good public relations towards David and his mother. Then on David's big day, his mother and other members of his family were invited to go to Wembley for the game with all expenses paid and a few pounds so that they wouldn't be out of pocket, all went well.

Sometime later England Boys were due to play Scotland Boys at Hampden Park, Glasgow. Frank Pickford was sent to see Mrs.Farrar to ask if she and any members of her family would like to go to the game. Upon his arrival at Mrs. Farrar's home he was met by an irate brother in-law who accused him of taking advantage of Mrs. Farrar and David, by inducing her and David to sign forms for Bolton before his fourteenth birthday, and in general, not being straight with them. He also added that David would not be joining Bolton at any time in the future and that the form they had signed should be torn up or returned immediately.

Although Bolton knew boys couldn't be signed to contracts before their fourteenth birthday, it was a general practice amongst most of the major clubs to do this, although, not always successful. Mrs. Farrar's brother in-law also handed Frank Pickford an envelope containing all the monies provided to the Farrar's on their day at Wembley, it was all expertly worked out in detail as if by an accomplished accountant. This was to be returned to Bill Ridding at Bolton who, not wanting to cause the boy any problems and perhaps to lose his Cap and International status, agreed to their request and subsequently dropped his interest in him and wished him well.

Mrs. Farrar was later accompanied by an unknown lady to Manchester Airport and flown to Scotland to watch David play for England, he later signed for Manchester United. I was upset to say the least, but now sufficiently aware of the rules. I'd learned a lesson.

Remarkably, at the same time as the Farrar escapade, a close friend of mine John Shore who was a Scout for West Bromwich Albion had spotted another lad, David Harrop who lived in the same block of flats as the Farrar boy. He also played for Manchester Boys and England Boys, and had been secured by John on a promise and a handshake that the Harrop lad would join West Brom upon leaving School, he too signed for Manchester United! A coincidence? I think perhaps not. Anyway, both boys failed to make the grade and were released before they were 18. John and I were very surprised by this as we felt they both had what it takes to be successful. Maybe their hearts weren't in it; they both went on to play in Non-League Football.

I began to find one or two useful lads who graced the 'A' and 'B' sides but unfortunately didn't quite make the professional ranks. These boys would come in and train one or two nights a week but were never taken on full time because of the economics of the club at that time.

Not many apprenticeships were available because of this. I'm sure that if full time coaching had been given to some of these boys, in particular local Hadfield lads Dennis Bardsley and Alan Doodson, they would have gone on to be as good as and perhaps better than most of the many full time Pro's, in particular Alan Doodson.

Alan was a good player in the Allan Clarke (Ex-Leeds and England) mold and with all the attributes required. He would have gone on to make it I'm sure, but for the continual interference of his dad, who was forever telling Bert Sproston (Ex-Manchester City and England Full-Back) who was Alan's coach, that his son wasn't getting treated as he wanted. Bert put up with his bickering for as long as he could and eventually told Mr.Doodson to take his son away. Alan left and returned to play in Amateur football dismayed and downhearted. I often see Alan, who is now in his forties, and if I could pay him a compliment it would be to say...

"You definitely would have made a good Pro my lad".

Not all youngsters with talent make it, for one reason or another. As in Alan Doodson's case, an interfering father. In most cases it's down to somones judgment, right or wrong. A lot of good young players have gone home disillusioned and dismayed at not making the grade. Some accepting the inevitable and getting on with their lives. Then there are others who go on to prove their judges wrong. Time has proven, over and over again, that top Managers and Coaches of high reputations, because of too early a judgment, have perhaps instilled in some youngster, a determination to prove a point. A perfect point in my opinion, being a young Alan Ball at Bolton Wanderers in 1953/54.

I had brought in a youngster about 17 years old for a trial at Bolton from Wythenshawe Lads Club; his name was Bevan Davies. I had watched the boy two or three times and thought he was a good prospect. Bolton was having a game at Hebden Bridge, which they often did. They sent a team of Apprentices and good prospects, as they did on many an occasion, in the hope of attracting a fair crowd that would help increase the Hebden Bridge funds. This particular game was on New Years day morning and Bolton's team included the boy I had recommended and a little red haired Alan Ball. That Bolton didn't consider good enough as a youngster.

"To small for the rigours of Top-Flight Football!" they said, but his determination to succeed proved them otherwise.

I was amazed at the skill of this young red headed dynamo. I thought my trialist was good, but he didn't quite measure up to young Alan. George Taylor said not to worry and that my lad might develop, he did eventually make it in the lower grades with Cambridge so my judgment hadn't been too far away. However, I had nominated three under-14 schoolboys for the summer trials and during my conversation with George about these boys, I learned that Bill Ridding was releasing Alan Ball. Bill Ridding thought that his smallish stature wouldn't be up to the rigours of Top-Flight Football. He was let go on a free to Blackpool and later sold on to Everton and then Arsenal. You know what happened from there on, he became one of the most influential players of our time.

I began to look at the standards I set for spotting. Alan was my ideal - Good first touch - Hard - Quick and brainy. I didn't let this deter me and I kept on searching regardless of who was judging my nominations. Time has proven, as I've said before, that mistakes will be made and judgments will inevitably be wrong from time to time.

People would ask me as I went about my Scouting, what it was that I looked for in the kids I was watching. I never had anything in particular that I looked for at first, but as I progressed I suppose what I looked for was.

A. Ability.

B. Intelligence.

C. Physical Condition

D. Attitude.

E. Character.

Not necessarily in that order but very important characteristics nonetheless. Ability is very important; a boy's natural skills allied to his physique and fitness are good basics for a start.

Unfortunately we aren't all built alike, a good big 'un' has an advantage, but a good little 'un' usually acquires other assets like - bravery and heart. Nothing appeals more to the Footballing public than watching a good little 'un' battling away against big 'uns'. Players like - Billy Bremner / Alan Ball / Nobby Stiles / Archie Gemmill / Bobby Collins and even today in the 90's we have Michael Owen. These are good examples of the determination and belief that the good little 'un' has in his own ability to be able to compete against the good big 'un'. There are plenty of these kind of players too numerous to mention.

Attitude, this in a youngster starting off in a career in football is most important. Any lad wanting to be a good professional will acquire the right attitude by working hard at his skills and not in hoping it will happen just because he is a good player. He needs to prepare well and not shirk his responsibilities and by doing this, he will build a character that will stand him in good stead against the setbacks and criticisms that will come his way.

He must be honest with himself in all that he is trying to do. The coaches and trainers who invariably are 'ex-players' and know all the tricks will eventually find out the cheats. If I can offer some advice to any young trialist –

1. Be honest
2. Have a belief in yourself
3. Never become complacent and 'big-headed'
4. Train hard and listen to advice constantly
5. Never be completely satisfied and look at what you are doing wrong and work on it to get it right.

Just remember that you and you alone listening to good advice - training and living correctly within the rigid disciplines laid down will, all going well, make it.

Bill Ridding

"Manager of Bolton Wanderers from 1951-58"

Alan Ball

"Not considered good enough, as a youngster"

Chapter 3

"On To Better Things"

As time went on I became more and more confident in my ability to spot good talent and felt I was ready to take on the likes of Manchester United and Arsenal 2and the other bigger clubs. I also thought, that if I was ready to take on the bigger clubs, I would need to be at a more progressive club, so I wrote to Don Revie at Leeds United who, I was led to believe, needed a representative in and around the Manchester area. Don was a little reticent to take me on at first because, at the time of writing to him, I had moved from Gorton to Hadfield, which was some 18 miles outside of Manchester. One of Don's assistants on the Scouting staff, Jeff Saunders, an Ex-Grammar School Headmaster, was impressed with my application and persuaded Don to take me on. I was now in a position to compete with the 'big boys' for the signatures of the talented schoolboys.

Working in conjunction with a chap called Alan Cowley, who ran a local Leeds junior side called Pudsey Juniors enabled me the chance to bring boys in for a game with his teams at various age levels. This was ideal because it also gave the people that mattered at Leeds the chance to see them at close hand. Among some of the boys I recommended at the under twelve age group, but subsequently not signed by Leeds United were - Andy Ritchie / Nicky Reid / Peter Coyne.

In the case of Andy Ritchie, he went on to play for Manchester United and Oldham and is currently Oldhams player manager. Nicky Reid had a successful career with Manchester City. Peter Coyne went on to play for Manchester Schoolboys and later joined

Manchester United as a schoolboy in 1973; he signed Pro'
forms in 1975 and was sold to Ashton United in 1977. I
felt sorry for Peter Coyne in that, his early days at United
were perhaps his undoing. His rejection of the tight
discipline controls necessary at professional level were
perhaps his downfall.

I think that it is extremely important to any
youngster with his foot on the first rung of the ladder to a
successful career, that he knuckle down and learn from
the onset to follow the very essential disciplines imposed
on him. It is very easy to become complacent. Being with
a professional club doesn't automatically mean you are a
professional, it is something you have to work hard at.
You should always look at what you might be doing
wrong and work at putting it right, it will, invariably,
improve your game.

I often think that if Peter Coyne had gone away to
a club from outside his home area he might have
benefited from it, by having to accept the disciplines more
readily. I'm not saying every boy should pack his bags
and move away from home, not every boy is alike, but
occasionally being away from mum and home comforts
does teach us to be harder and more independent.

So far my emphasis has been on the schoolboy
scene, but I have also been involved rummaging around
the Pro/Amateur ranks. Whilst at Leeds United I was
asked to go and have a look at a young lad playing for
Rhyl against Skelmersdale at Skelmersdale. It was on a
Thursday night, August 28th.1969. I had no car at the
time and a Referee friend of mine Brian Price volunteered
to take me. The Rhyl team was run ragged by a very
good Skelmersdale side, whom I thought at the time,
were the best non-league side around. They outplayed

Rhyl and the young lad I'd come to have a look at didn't impress, instead my eye was drawn to their winger who had an outstanding performance scoring 2 goals playing on alternative wings. Skelmersdale, had at that time, 4 or 5 lads who went on to play in the Pro-Ranks. Their Chairman Bill Gregson in 1971, with his strong desire to win, got caught making illegal payments to his players and was severely reprimanded and fined £1500 by the powers that be and subsequently suspended. This cost Bill dearly for some time to follow.

Maurice Edeleston, who was manager of Third Division Mansfield at that time was there also, he was obviously making inquiries about the young winger. I'd not heard of the lad before that night and went back to Leeds with a glowing report recommending the youngster as a great prospect and that other clubs were showing an interest also. Incidentally Manchester City had him, but never retained him on amateur forms because he was studying for his degree at Warwick University. I thought he would be ideal for Leeds as a replacement for Eddie Gray who was coming up to retirement, but no one at Leeds seemed bothered about taking him on. The fact that Manchester City hadn't bothered retaining his signature suggested to the Leeds cynics that maybe something was amiss.

Some weeks later the young winger came to Buxton with Skelmersdale in a Cheshire League game and was outstanding again and scored another couple of goals. I sent in another glowing report and again nothing happened. A couple of weeks after that, Matt McPeak, who was the Leeds Scout on merseyside and unaware of my earlier reports, saw the young winger play and sent in a report saying that he was a great prospect and recommended that Don Revie and his assistant Maurice Lindley should have a look at him S.A.P. When they finally did in March 1970, Bill Gregson told Maurice Lindley that he was to late! He had just signed for Liverpool. The young winger's name was Steve Heighway.

Time eventually proved in my belief that he would become a top professional. I got a lot of self-satisfaction in that and also in my belief that I could spot a good player amongst the Pro/Amateur ranks. I also thought that my reports on Steve Heighway should have been processed much quicker than they were. Again we look at judgment and wonder what if. Steve went on to play for Liverpool for ten years winning, 2 European Cup Winners and 2 UEFA Cup Winners Medals, 4 League Championships and I F.A.Cup Winners Medal and played 34 times for The Republic of Ireland. The importance on acting quickly on information received, is a lesson to be learned.

Working for Leeds during their peak years was a great honour indeed and, in all fairness, working for Don Revie was an even greater honour. All who worked for him were given a fair reward and respect for all the hard work they did. Don, was castigated by the press for the way he resigned from the England job, the truth he never fully managed to reveal. He would have been the biggest fool in the World to have waited to be sacked. He decided to make the move to the Arab Emirates because, their offer was not only financial stability for himself and his family, but total control to construct and develop the Football, as he wished, with a completely free hand. This he was denied by the beaurocrats at the Football Association. He was a great 'boss' to work for and he treated everyone with equal respect, from the cleaners, groundsmen, to players alike, he got the same respect in return.

Don took over at Leeds, four days after Jack Taylor resigned. Just prior to Don taking over as player manager at Leeds, Bournemouth had contacted them, about Don's availability. Chairman, Harry Reynolds, drafted a letter to Bournemouth, agreeing to their approach and recommending Don to them. Fortunately for Leeds, he changed his mind, realizing that Don would be the ideal man for them. He destroyed the letter and convinced the board to agree to Don's appointment. Little knowing, that he would transform them from a mediocre Second Division Club, into one of Europe's finest.

Don was a humble man, very kind and sincere. He was never to big to find time for anyone, he even had an extension built on to his house, so that two elderly aunts could be closer to the family at a time when they needed, because of their age, that extra security. This showed his humility and what a soft centre he had. Another of Don's great attributes, was his accessibility to anyone on his staff. He was very basic and down to earth. He would always find time for a talk or discussion with you on any matter, wether important, or trivial. He would never keep you waiting long, or until it suited him, that wasn't Don. A request for an interview with him, was usually the same day. He always made you feel at ease when discussing whatever subject, be it about a player, a constructive criticism, or a personal complaint. One didn't carry a problem around, or brood about it. He never changed his grass roots attachments; he was very understanding and compassionate in so many ways. He was a deep thinker too and, always sought to conquer every problem.

I once remarked to Don, about his handling of his great players, Bremner, Giles, Lorrimer and Charlton. I said that they must have given him many a headache, as they progressed through the ranks into becoming the great players they did. I asked about Billy Bremner in particular and, was he a difficult lad to bring through, with his volatile temper and all? Don pondered...

"Yes!" he replied "He was, early on! He seemed to lose his early promise and his form dipped".

Don said he began to wonder if something wasn't amiss, and thought he might have a solution. He told me that, one day after Billy had finished training with the other apprentices, that he wanted to see him in his office. As soon as he was changed and, wondering what was wrong, Billy reported to the 'gaffers' office, it was almost Lunchtime. Don said...

"We are going for your clothes at your digs!"

Billy was taken aback and obviously upset. He was wondering what he had done. Don said...

"Pack a bag and back to the car!"

Upset and confused, Billy asked where they were going? Don said...

"I'm taking you home for a few days break!"

Don had sensed that Billy was a bit homesick and missing his 'girlfriend', who I believe, later became his wife. Don drove Billy home to enjoy an unheralded break with his family and girlfriend. Don then added...

"I will pick you up at the weekend, and then I want to see the real Billy Bremner, back to his best, and wanting to play by showing me my early judgment of you".

Billy never let Don down and, from that moment on -

'The Gaffer could walk on water'.

Human, understanding, humility, Don had it all. I think all his lads eventually recognised this, though seeming too gentle at times. He created a harmony and unity second to none.

I remember another occasion, much later on. I had the good fortune to be having Sunday lunch with Don, after a bruising encounter with Man United the previous day. I asked him if they infuriated him at times, in their playing possession football, retaining the ball in the penalty area when under pressure. He said of course he did, and that he remonstrated with them at the half-time break, but all he got in return was, his hair ruffled by Billy Bremner, who told Don to...

"Stop worrying! We kept the ball didn't we? If we have it, they can't score! So stop worrying".

That was the extent of the 'ticking' off.

His managerial career at Leeds, got off to a slow start and they only just avoided relegation to the Third Division in 1962. Don was also a patient man. Not one to panic. Don knew what he wanted and set out his stall for the future, by spending time developing all the good work left behind by Jack Taylor and his Youth policy, with players such as, Gary Sprake, Paul Heaney and Norman Hunter, who became part of the successful side that won the Division Two Title in 1964. He did this, by developing a 'family' type of unit with everyone connected with the Club, from senior players down to the juniors. He treated one and all with equal respect.

Don was very successful at Leeds because of this. During his time at Leeds, Don was named Manager of the Year in, 1969, 1970 and 1972; he was also awarded the O.B.E. in 1970. He could have joined Everton as Manager in 1973, but stayed on and won another title. A truly great Manager, but he eventually decided that, things couldn't go on the way they were forever and, he quit to take up the England manager's job after thirteen successful years with Leeds.

On certain occasions, about two or three times during the season, usually when Leeds had a home game on the Saturday, all the Scouts and representatives of Leeds United and their wives of course, including those from Scotland, Wales and Ireland, were sent invitations for an overnight stay at the Faversham Hotel in Leeds. Scouts could also invite any boys they felt worth a trial. They too, would be invited to watch the game on the Saturday and, obviously, play in the trial game on the Sunday. They too, would also be invited to enjoy the hospitality of Roger Quillam and his wife at their Faversham Hotel. After an evening meal, myself and another Scout or Scouts, would take the boys Ten-Pin Bowling and then back to the Hotel for bed by 10.00pm. The other Scouts, and myself would then enjoy a pint or two whilst ensuring no 'villains' broke house rules.

On the Sunday morning after breakfast, we would all go to the training ground, where a game was organised for all the trialists. Most of the Scouts and parents were there and, invariably, Don Revie also. He would mix and chat with as many parents and Scouts as was possible. I remember one occasion when Don, wasn't happy with the way the boys were being instructed to play. At that time, formation Football was just creeping in to Schoolboy Football 4-4-2 4-2-4 4-3-3. Instructions were being given to the boys that was stemming individual expression. In this particular game, I had two boys from different Counties, Cheshire and Staffordshire. They were being asked to play in a restricted area, playing in what we term today as Mid-Field. They were being asked to patrol and control the area just in front of their defenders, and up to the opposing penalty area. They were also asked not to encroach in other areas by the coaches.

Don wasn't happy with what he was seeing and listening to. He then asked the Referee to stop the game. He went on to the pitch to talk to the boys, who were obviously, playing within themselves because of the restrictions being imposed. He asked them what was the problem. They told him it was the new formations they were being asked to play. Don told them to forget all that and go and enjoy themselves, so that everyone watching could enjoy themselves also. He also said...

"My Scouts told me that you all could play, go out there and show us".

That was Don Revie, he wasn't just the First Team Manager.

I would like to point out that, after leaving Leeds to join Manchester City and, until Alan Ball came as Manager, I don't think I ever saw a Manager, in some twenty odd years, grace a touch line to watch young trialists play. It isn't a great deal to ask and, I know first team pressures are a priority, but I haven't seen many today that compare to the humble Don Revie. He once came with me to Wythenshawe Manchester when Leeds were top of Division One, to personally sign Gary Felix. I'd asked Don if he could find the time to come and use his influence in convincing the boy to sign for Leeds. This he did and, the Felix family was so overwhelmed at his down to earth attitude. Gary didn't make it all the way to the top, but I don't think he would have forgotten that occasion.

After the Sunday morning trial game, when we were all together, to chat and talk shop, Don and his staff came along to have a few words with us all. To thank us for our efforts and as always, as a gesture to our lady wives, they would invariably take home some nice little gift, a bottle of Perfume or a box of Chocolates, this was a

Don Revie touch. You were always made to feel a part of every success. When Leeds won the Championship in season 1968/69 my wife and I received a Gold and Gilt adorned card inviting us to join the celebrations at the Queens Hotel in Leeds and after the celebrations we again stayed overnight at the Faversham Hotel. This was only the beginning of great celebratory nights with Leeds.

Whilst I was there, Leeds made three appearances at Wembley for games against - Chelsea - Arsenal and Sunderland. Each time the team got to Wembley so did all the Scouts and their wives. We were treated and taken care of as well as any of the players or members of the staff. All we had to do was turn up, prior to the Final, at The Faversham Hotel on the Friday night for another enjoyable overnight stay. We would have an early morning cup of tea and off to the Railway Station for an 8.00am 'Special Train' to Paddington Station London. A typical British Rail journey with a typical British Rail breakfast. We then went by coach to our Hotel, usually the Russell or the Imperial. We would only have time for a quick 'wash and brush up', then on to a buffet lunch fit for a King, then we were on our way to the greatest Footballing scene one can ever take part in.

The coach made it's way down Wembley way and into the private car-park, it was only a short walk to the entrance where we stood and watched the crowds descending on Wembley Stadium singing and waving their team colours. Television does a great job of showing this, but there is nothing quite like the atmosphere of actually being there. It's simply breathtaking.

My wife Lily was quite overcome by it all. On her first occasion, the game against Chelsea in 1969, she said she felt embarrassed and suggested that she wait outside and let some youngster go in with her ticket. I nevertheless persuaded her that she belonged and deserved to be there. Once inside she became more at ease and in the end was cheering as wildly as all the other 99.999 people packed inside this great Stadium. The game ended 2-2 - we lost the replay 2-1.

That evening we were wined and dined at the Cafe Royal, what an experience this was, my wife and I were a little apprehensive, we had never been to anything quite like this before. Within minutes of arriving we were all at ease and enjoying ourselves because of the efficient way the evening was planned by Don and his associates.

The players arrived at the same time and soon we were all mixing and talking and partaking in the 'Free' liquid refreshment, not abused I might add. During the evening I had the distinct pleasure of a brief chat with the wonderful Matt Busby. I inquired as to his health. He said to me...

"You're a Manchester lad and you're Scouting for Leeds! How come?".

I told him I was just seeking to get a job within the game and that I had applied to both Manchester Clubs and was turned down, but I'd achieved my objective at Leeds thanks to Jeff Saunders and Don Revie who were looking for someone to cover the Manchester area.

The dinner was something to be seen to be believed and at each ladies place setting there was a small gift (again a Don Revie touch). There were a few speeches and toasts and a song from Ronnie Hilton. As the evening went on I was gasping for a 'beer'. I saw Jack Charlton enjoying a glass and I asked him as to its source? He replied...

"Just summon a waiter and ask for some".

I did so and the Waiter brought a huge jug that must have held about 4 or 5 pints. I did my best to do it justice.

Then Lily and I headed back to the Hotel for a few hours sleep.

We were back again in season 1971/72 for the final against Arsenal that Leeds won 1-0, and we enjoyed another great stay at the Faversham in Leeds, also at the Russell in London, with an equally great evening. The celebrations on the train on the way home were amazing, the champagne flowed and the Cup was passed around and a good time, was had by all. We were back yet again the next year for the 1972/73 final against Sunderland and we all know what happened then! A 1-0 defeat. Although we'd been defeated the celebrations were as glorious as the others were and enjoyable nonetheless.

On the Sunday before we left for home we had a couple of hours to spare so I took my wife on a shopping trip to Petticoat Lane. I'd always promised her we would do this if the occasion arose and if you haven't done this then you haven't lived. There is nothing anywhere in the world to compare. All the different stalls with every nationality in their traditional dress. The 'cockney spivs' were doing their typical brand of dealing. It's a simply amazing place. Whilst my wife Lily was shopping for some lingerie for our daughter, who was fourteen at the time, I spotted out of the corner of my eye this mop of blond hair and as I turned I noticed this huge man, he was built like a 'brick shit-house'. I thought to myself...

"I know this bloke!"

Sure enough, when he turned round, I could see it was my old Army pal from my time in Benghazi in 1949. I hadn't seen him for all these years, yet he was unmistakable. His name was Jimmy 'Geordie' James. It was a good thing we bumped into him, as we were about to leave, otherwise I don't think I would have been sober for the entire weekend, as we often were during our time in Benghazi.

I recall one time when Jimmy and I had saved a few quid and we decided to go for a real 'piss-up' in downtown Benghazi. We dressed in civilian clothes and went to this Club that was only frequented by Officers and Warrant Officers. We were enjoying ourselves and had a few drinks, from which, we became a little boisterous to say the least, it all ended with us getting arrested for impersonating senior CO's. I was fortunate in that my CO was a lenient man, and no charges were brought, otherwise I might have lost my corporals stripes.

Jimmy was a character / Footballer / Boxer / Singer / 'Goon' and poor scholar, but spoke Arabic better than the Libyans themselves. He had great abilities but didn't always use them right, he hated disciplines, but eventually, Army life, taught him to live with them. At football he tried to imitate the late great Len Shackleton 'The Clown Prince' of soccer. Jimmy was a crowd pleaser and tried to do so on every occasion.

I also remember one game where the goal-keeper kicked the ball high in the air and as it came down Jimmy didn't try to trap it in the normal manner, he anticipated the bounce and trapped it with his back-side by sitting on it as it hit the ground, which was a feat in itself, then in the same instant he would jump up and majestically pass it, all in one movement. Len Shackleton would have been proud of this it was so graceful. Jimmy had watched 'Shack' do it many times and copied him. Incidentally, my wife Lil and I had a 'great time' down Petticoat Lane.

Don Revie

"A humble man"

Sir Matt Busby

"Sir Matt joined Manchester City on February 11th 1928, and played 202 times for them scoring eleven goals. He took over at United in February 1945 as Manager. He went on to develop the most successful club in England. Survived the Munich Air crash. Then went on to realise his dream by winning the European Cup in 1968. Sir Matt retired at the end of that season. Sadly, Sir Matt passed away on January 20th 1994. A truly wonderful man"

Chapter 4

"Time For A Change!"

A change was underway at Leeds. In 1974 Don Revie was appointed manager of the England team and Brian Clough became Leeds United's new manager. Unfortunately not for long though, his reign lasted 42 days. He just didn't fit. The players wanted Don Revie and the 'Family' he had created. Brian Clough then went on to glory with Nottingham Forest and to win the European Cup not only once, but twice. I'm sure all of this could have been Leeds United. I would have loved to have worked for him, he is a man who knew what he wanted and knew how to get it by commanding respect from Directors and players alike.

After Brian Clough came Jimmy Armfield. I didn't think he would succeed either, I felt he didn't have the mental toughness of a Revie or a 'Cloughy', I was sure he wouldn't be able to handle the Board or the players. Before Don left he appointed Tony Collins as Chief Scout, he was, at the time, assistant manager at Bristol City. He was a likable chap, but in my estimation not very authoritative and offered little or no resistance to new club policies (economics) introduced after Brian Clough's departure. Although the changes were not very significant they would mean a financial change in the expenses structure, particularly for the Scouts. I was thinking more along the lines of an increase not a deduction!. We worked very hard and with a lot of dedication and I felt we deserved a little more.

I made my feelings known to Tony Collins and told him that if the changes became effective, I would have to leave. I'd had one or two offers from other clubs offering better terms. I had been developing quite a good name and reputation and I felt that joining another club would have no adverse affect on my scouting in general. I informed Tony Collins of my intentions and told him that being that I had no binding contract I would move on.

Around October/November 1974, Steve Fleet, who was at that time, Youth Team Coach at Manchester City and knowing I was no longer involved at Leeds, suggested I join Manchester City. I'd known Steve since the late 60's when he was endeavouring to do an almost impossible job as Youth Coach - Scout and anything else that needed doing at Stockport County, who were battling with ecomomics even then. He also developed a great player or two; one he pulled out of the hat at Stockport was Paul Hart. Paul went on to play for Blackpool / Leeds and Nottingham Forest, where he is their Youth Development Officer at present day. Tony Book was the current manager and Ken Barnes was chief Scout at Maine Road. Ken had taken over from Harry Godwin and Tony Book had taken over from Ron Saunders. Tony was, before becoming manager at City, a very popular and successful player during the period from 1967-70. He was voted Player of the Year in 1969, jointly held with Dave Mackay of Derby County.

Tony did a tremendous job as manager turning City into a highly successful side before being replaced by Malcolm Alison in 1979. The City board felt we needed a more 'high profile' manager to help fuel their obsessive need to better Manchester United. I didn't have a great deal of contact with Tony, his prime objective was obviously with first and reserve team matters. He was very much interested in the progress of the younger players, but kept his contact with the younger element through Ken Barnes and Steve Fleet.

I said I would consider joining them and would let Ken know of my decision as soon as I could. I thought about it for a short time and then phoned Ken and asked for a meeting to discuss my joining City as a Scout. I went along to meet Ken and Tony Book at Maine Road on December 28th.1974. City Reserves were playing Blackburn Rovers. I was asked as to what my terms were at Leeds. They offered me a fair increase and an assurance that I would not lose out in any way. My status at City, although only a verbal agreement, was to be more or less as deputy to Ken Barnes.

I was introduced to the staff and they were instructed to meet my needs whatever they were should Ken not be available, so the next stage of my Scouting career began. This was a great opportunity for me to be able to roll up my sleeves and get stuck in. Ken was very pleased with my work and the assistance I gave to him. In his early days in the job, deskwork wasn't Ken's strong point and I was able to give useful advice particularly on Schoolboy procedures.

I began to enjoy it so much, that I was devoting nearly all my spare time to Manchester City outside of my work at British Aerospace where I was a Draftsman Technician. I was also appointed as Chairman of the works Committee D.A.T.A. the Draftsman / Technicians Union. My life was becoming fully booked up, so much so that it got to the stage where I never booked any annual holidays until I checked the Football schedules e.g. July / August - Christmas / Easter trials etc. City initially only ran Junior sides from the under-12 age group and upwards, although Junior Soccer was gaining in momentum and under-10 and under-11 Leagues were beginning to be introduced. It was about this time that Barry Bennall arrived in Manchester from London. His talent for organising and coaching was heralded as something different.

Bennall approached the club via Ken Barnes to undertake the coaching and creating junior sides. His initial set-up consisted of local Manchester Amateur Football enthusiasts, people like Dave Norman, a big rough diamond who was a capable but likable man. Dave helped to create a stable organised set-up, which became a household name in and around Manchester in the recruitment of the best young talent. City rented an excellent facility from the Cheadle and District Council at Park Road, Cheadle; this enabled them to provide two good playing pitches with dressing room facilities. Although used primarily by our reserve and Youth Teams, it was the ideal location for our up and coming junior sides. It was ideal also in that, during the lighter nights, it provided somewhere for training, we also used it on Sundays for trial games etc.

Barry Bennall was about twenty years old when he came to Manchester from Barnes in London. He very quickly set up and established a very good local Football Team, which he named 'Senrab' after the district he came from in London, which was Barnes in reverse! It later became known as Whitehill Juniors. The Club didn't take long in earning the reputation of being one of the better clubs representing boys from the ages of 10 - 13.

Bennall recruited and trained these boys and both parents and boys alike admired his coaching techniques. His reputation as a coach began to spread and the Club began to attract the better players in these age groups, they were all very committed to him as a coach and everyone agreed, that he was exactly that, a very good coach.

I think that the majority of us at Manchester City and all those who were associated with Whitehill Juniors or 'Senrab', were taken in and let down by this very talented young man, who was so gifted, with an ability to teach youngsters on how to use their Football skills. Hundreds of people and almost all the kids who played for him trusted him. Suspicions about him were aired on many an occasion, but inquiries about his behaviour never revealed his Paedophiliac mentality until it was to late.

How sad and distasteful it was. I only hope that the boys and their parents who suffered will forgive us in that we too, were beguiled and hoodwinked by this terrible person. I am confident that the new guidelines and the moral codes now being set by the Governing bodies, will hopefully, never allow this sort of thing to happen again to parents and boys who put their trust in us.

Bennall was convicted of a total of nineteen offences committed against young boys between 1978 and 1992. This all came about after reports came to light, that he had been arrested and imprisoned for sex offences committed whilst in Florida, USA. On his release from prison in the USA, and his subsequent return to England, he was then charged and imprisoned for the offences committed between 1978 and 1992.

I would just like to point out at this juncture, that whilst most of us at Manchester City, including those responsible for the enhancement of Junior Football, were held in awe at the coaching ability of Barry Bennall. Youth Team Coach Steve Fleet did not ever accept him as a person or coach, reserving his judgment. He just did not accede to acknowledging Bennall in any way and I must respect Steve's long-term judgment, never ever did he have anything to do with Bennall. Ken and I tried to bridge the gap, but to no avail.

The basic Junior set-up began to produce a good standard of boys, and along with the recommendations of other boys from our out of town Scouts, we began holding trial games bringing in the boys from all over Lancashire, Yorkshire, Derbyshire, Scotland, Wales and later from Ireland. This allowed Ken to be more selective over boys he thought would be capable of apprenticeships.

We held the trials usually during School-Breaks e.g. Easter/August Holidays - end of season and sometimes around the December breaks. The harsh English winters of the seventies and eighties defeated most of our plans on bringing in the Scottish / Welsh and Irish lads around the Xmas break. Nonetheless, Ken Barnes and Steve Fleet began to produce a really good crop of top class players that came through the ranks in the 70's and 80's, some achieved stardom and first team status at City and subsequently at other Clubs later in their careers, namely...

Peter Barnes	1974-79	Tony Henry	1974-81
Gary Owen	1974-79	Paul Power	1974-86
Dave Bennett	1976-81	Ray Ranson	1976-84
Nicky Reid	1977-87	Tommy Caton	1979-83
Garry Bennett	1979-81	Steve Kinsey	1979-86
Clive Wilson	1979-87	Geoff Lomax	1981-85
Paul Simpson	1982-88	Earl Barratt	1983-87
Paul Moulden	1984-89	David White	1984-93
Andy Hinchcliffe	1985-90	Paul Lake	1985-89
Ian Brightwell	1986-98	Paul Warhurst	1986-88

Gerry Taggart 1987-90   David Brightwell 1988-95
Michael Hughes1988-92

Not to mention the likes of...

John Foster	David Kerr
Steve Lomas	Ade Mike
Richard Edgehill	Rae Ingram
Ged Kielty	Geoff Clarke
Andy May	Eric Nixon
Jamie Hoyland	Jason Beckford
Darren Beckford	Ian Scott
Steve Redmond	Neil Lennon
Mike Sheron	Chris Coleman
Ashley Ward	Ian Crooks
John Beresford	Gary Flitcroft

All of these boys have gone on to play first team Football at one time or another, wether at City or at another Club. Some are still competing at the top level even today, even in our troubled 90's, we were still turning out good quality players that came through our Youth set up.

I doubt that any other Football Club has brought so many youngsters through to play in their first team, only to be sold on. At least 75% of these players have had, or are still having, good careers at other clubs.

And now our current crop of youngsters making steady progress through the ranks at the present time, with regular first and reserve team duties...

Nicky Fenton	Rhys Day
Lee Crooks	Gary Mason
Leon Mike	Steve Hodgson
Shaun Wright-Phillips	Terry Dunfield
Jeff Whiteley	etc.etc...

I could go on listing prospects right down to our under nines. The future looks good for City and deservedly so for it's faithful supporters.

1979 saw the return of City's 'Prodigal Son' Malcolm Alison. It also was the beginning of a succession of managers over the next twenty years!. Malcolm became overall in charge of coaching and first team affairs, to quote Malcolm he said...

"I'm not just a coach, I'm a scientist!.".

'Great Expectations' heralded his arrival and major changes were introduced and the club was split in two, with those in favour retained, those against were up for grabs. This was a calamity in my opinion and the beginning of our downward spiral.

New signings were brought in at immense cost with no success. Chairman Peter Swales, normally a very shrewd financial businessman was persuaded, I believe, into spending money as if it were monopoly money with sorties into the transfer market on very expensive failures. The Chairman, along with his Board of Directors, finally decided in 1980, that Malcolm's reign should end, as they could see no light at the end of the tunnel, with City precariously clinging on to a place in the old First Division.

Chapter 5

"Just call me 'Boss'"

After Malcolm Alison we saw a stream of Managers who came and went with a consistent regularity, first was John Bond. John was persuaded to move from Norwich City to take over from Malcolm and steady the 'Rocking Boat'. John arrived at Maine Road with his entourage and in his first meeting with the players he instructed them to...

" Just call me 'Boss' ".

A good start.

John brought with him his full compliment of staff from Norwich namely, John Benson as his Assistant Manager. John Sainty came as his first team Coach and an ex-colleague of John Bond's, Tony Scott, who'd retired from playing due to injury and was at that time working as a Butcher, was brought in as the Youth Team coach.

Tony Scott would replace Steve Fleet, who the previous season had taken the Youth Team, to the Final of the Youth Cup for the first time ever. Steve Fleet was also responsible for the progress of Peter Barnes to first team stardom, and with helping Paul Power / Ged Keegan / Kenny Clements / Tony Henry and John Beresford maintain their steady progress to first team status. Steve recruited John Beresford personally. He further helped along the way Roger Palmer / Ashley Ward / Jamie Hoyland and Gary Owen to achieve their 'goals'. These were the 70's and 80's lad's who cost City nothing. Steve's reward was to be replaced by Tony Scott, a Butcher.

Tony was a nice enough man. He smartened the kids up by changing their mode of dress and made them get 'nice' haircuts, plus adding firm disciplines. I didn't escape his disciplines either. I was rebuked for using 'foul language' in the dressing room whilst encouraging the lads during a Youth Cup game against United, it was only intended as a 'gee up', but Tony felt it was out of place. I think in the end, common sense told Tony that he was struggling to fill the bill and he resigned to take up Church work in Australia.

I, along with all the other Scouts was invited to a Scouts meeting. John Bond and his new Management Team wanted to air their intentions and plans for City's future. I felt that the move to City, was a significant move up in the World for them, but no benefits would be forthcoming to any of us after listening to their poorly prepared outlined intentions.

Finances were tight, we understood that, but I for one had not had any expenses for the last three months, I put no blame on Ken Barnes or Bernard Halford for that, just the circumstances of the clubs resources at that point in time. Then from a lot of expounded ideas they issued to us, came a suggestion, by them, the management team, that Scouts would be paid in an entirely different way to that in the past. A sum of 10/12 pence per mile for journeys to games from their home plus still having the facility of obtaining 2/3 or 4 gallons of petrol, getting a receipt and submitting it along with your reports on whatever day you normally submitted them for a refund. The Scouting network that covered Junior and Schoolboy Football were then told that Management had appointed a Ted Davies to Youth Development Officer. I wasn't happy with this arrangement.

I first came in touch with Ted Davies whilst I was still at Leeds United, he was running a Junior side from

Manchester called 'Mercer Celtic'.   In my dealings with him, I felt that he was a person I couldn't trust and after leaving Leeds and joining Manchester City, I felt I must try and dissuade Ken Barnes from taking him on as a Scout.   I believed that Ted Davies had a poor image in Manchester Junior soccer circles, he was, in my opinion, ruthless and very dogmatic in his approach at times.   I also felt that he was too ambitious and very objective in his intent to attain a senior post in Football, regardless of who or what stood in his way.

I remember him once asking me if I had any pretensions of becoming Chief Scout at City. I replied stating that...

"I was happy with the role I had" albeit a part-time role.

Ted's ambitions began to develop with the arrival of John Bond, by being appointed Youth Development Officer, as I have stated.   I also believed that he attempted to undermine Ken's position by spreading false rumours, but this misfired and he was eventually dismissed. Ken, initially thought that Ted Davies had ability and deserved a chance, almost to Ken's regret.

I initially addressed the Management at this meeting to say that, none but a fool would accept the intended method of paying expenses and I could not accept this and that I would resign.   I also said that this unpalatable appointment, (Ted Davies) would never be accepted by me. That I had accepted a gentleman's agreement, on the shake of a hand, with Ken Barnes and Tony Book, in accepting conditions similar to those I'd had previously with Leeds United and Don Revie, therefore I would submit my resignation in writing.

This I did over the weekend and I posted it registered mail with copies to Peter Swales / John Bond /

John Benson / John Sainty and asking for payments outstanding and my intention to sever my links with Manchester City. I received a phone call from John Benson on the Tuesday morning the day after they had received my letter of resignation. He asked me if I would come in and meet him to talk it over. I agreed to this and made arrangements to meet with him on Thursday at noon. Tony Scott the new Youth Team coach who said he would like to discuss the matter with me met me. I said that with no disrespect to him I preferred to talk the matter over with John Benson. John was in the Gymnasium playing head-tennis?

I said that I would wait ten minutes for him and if he didn't come I would return to my place of employment at British Aerospace. He finally came and said he didn't want to accept my resignation and that I had done a first class job and that they wanted me to continue. I emphatically refused to be answerable to Ted Davies. This he tried hard to cajole me into accepting, but I still refused. The Management's plan was for Ken Barnes to do the Pro-Side of the Scouting and Ted Davies to do the Youth. At least this was their intention; I still refused to be answerable to Ted Davies.

We eventually compromised in that I would, for a short time, be answerable to John Benson. I was 'cheeky' enough to ask for my expenses arrears, John said he would take care of it and a few days later I received a cheque for two thirds of what I was owed, which was most welcome. For a short while Ken had to suffer the injustice of sharing his office with Ted Davies the new Youth Development Officer. He also began to wonder about his own future. Rumours were rampant, but 'fortune favours the brave' as they say, when quite suddenly, a wind of change blew in Kens face as he was informed that the newly appointed Youth Development

Officer would be dispensed with forthwith. Ken, rightfully restored continued as Chief Scout and lived to see the Bond era plod unsuccessfully through 1980-83. When John took over, City were hovering precariously near the foot of Division 1. City eventually being relegated to Division 2 for the first time since 1966. It's a tough old game this Football business.

Billy McNeil came down from Scotland in 1983 to try and restore City to its former glory. He got us back into the First Division, but failed to develop anything significant and, he walked out in 1986 to join Aston Villa. His reason for doing so, was a lack of finance. He later admitted that he was wrong to leave City for Villa in 1986. Around this time, Ken asked me if I would be interested in working alongside him in order to ease the workload. The City Management offered me a £100.00 per week, an offer I had to refuse as I was earning around £140.00 per week at my job with British Aerospace. I suggested to Ken that perhaps an alternative of seeking a part-time assistant for 2/3 days a week. This would help in offloading a lot of the Junior Soccer and F.A. correspondence. I felt it may interest one of our newcomer Scouts Terry Farrell.

Terry was a true 'blue' who had been invalided out of the Fire Service. He was very bright and conversant on everyday junior soccer activities. Terry would be a more than useful acquisition as he had had a lot of success in Junior Soccer with his Flixton Junior Team. He would be leaving behind a side that had gone unbeaten for three seasons.
His local knowledge was invaluable and he passed on to City some good prospects. Ken took Terry on to deal primarily with the Scouting of Junior soccer.

Terry watched, listened and learned and availed himself of the workings of Junior Scouting and eventually as the job grew in size, he was fully acknowledged as the Youth Development Officer.   The otherwise part-time job now became a full-time role.

Jimmy Frizzell was then appointed manager, albeit briefly until the end of season 1987 when City were once again relegated.

Mel Machin was next to be appointed, and he got us back into the First Division at the end of season 1988/89, but things didn't go to well early in the campaign, and once again, with us struggling near the foot of the table, his tenure as manager was terminated, even after beating the 'old enemy' United at Maine Road 5-1.

Mel was a nice person, and was liked by the majority of supporters, but he was fully occupied with first team problems. This led to neglect in Youth growth, and a lack of funds to sustain further progress with the Clubs Youth policies, just at a time when we needed to maintain the momentum we had gathered with our successes from the late 70's and early 80's. The Paul Lake era and our Youth successes were beginning to fail. Failure at Boardroom level in funding a youth policy restricted us in our efforts to maintain a level challenge with our neighbours from Old Trafford.

Howard Kendal then superceded Mel for a brief spell in 1989-90. I must say that I never but once made his aquaintance and of course Peter Reid replaced him from 1990/93. All these changes didn't make Scouting any easier. New Management meant new ideas - new ideas meant new policies and new ways of doing things, it didn't help.

Peter Reid, nonetheless, was Peter Reid. Like him or hate him, Peter was an honest and forthright man. He sent me a note thanking me for my past services to the club and that I was no longer needed for Scouting in the Pro-Ranks, as he was bringing in his own men. He added that he had received good reports on my Scouting in the Junior and Schoolboy ranks and he hoped that I would continue, in this role.

Peter began to set out his stall and amongst his entourage was Sam Ellis as his Assistant, Ken Barnes job was to be given to Bobby Saxton and Jack Chapman a role in Youth Development. Jack had had a role as Chief Scout at Bury and at Blackpool. He was a good and capable man who had had many years' experience. He was to be situated with Terry Farrell, without title, though not in status. He was earmarked by Peter Reid to take over on Junior Football. Jack was a more than capable man, very experienced. He had the ability and the connections, a good judge of football talent, proven and tested. He was also a good communicator who commanded respect with his cheerful, optimistic and honest approach. He was willing to listen to others viewpoints, an obvious choice for the job, in my estimation.

What little time Jack spent in this role, was a pleasant surprise to all the scouts. In particular when he invited all to attend Schoolboy and Junior trial matches. We were asked to take an active part in the trials. We were given team sheets with all the boy's names, and asked to express our own viewpoints on all the participants. After the games were over, we were asked to stay for a 'cuppa', which I was designated to make, and throw your hat in the ring and have your say. This was a winner of respect from all of the Scouts present, a recognition, but it enabled Jack to digest the various opinions expressed and give a majority opinion of the player's abilities. A good constructive exercise, misfortune was, whilst this initial and welcome change to Youth Procedure was being introduced, Peter Reid was beginning to experience difficulties at boardroom level.

Pressures were being exerted on him from the Chairman and Directors to make changes with his management team, these pressures he would not yield to. He was asked to remove Sam Ellis, his assistant. Sam's brusque and offhanded manners were offending those at the top, which he had scant regard for. Peter would not bow to this intimidation, and would sooner leave City than submit to pressure. Peter did a good job, and was held in high regard by his players and supporters alike, but he was not ideally a Directors man, he was perhaps too frank and forthright and he defended his team selections even when unpalatable. Although he steered the team to reasonable League positions, having spent very little in acquiring the players he brought in, he was duly passed on in 1993. Another huge setback, chaos was once more thrust on the long-suffering fans, who pondered what next?

Perhaps preponderant, but when Peter Swales announced that Brian Horton, who was managing at Oxford United, a complete managerial unknown, was to be brought in to succeed Peter Reid, eye brows were raised, Footballing manuals were scanned questioning his pedigree, was he the one? He again was as nice a person as one could wish to meet, he made no radical changes and appointed Jimmy Frizzell as Chief Scout and leaving Terry Farrell in his role as Youth Development Officer, eventually dispatching Jack Chapman as surplus to requirements. Jack returned to Blackpool as Chief Scout.

Jimmy then regrouped his Scouts including former Scouts such as Ken Barnes to do their previous Pro-Scouting, including myself occasionally.

Brian polite and undemanding, kept himself fully occupied with his first team duties and rarely ventured into the needs and wants of the ever-growing World of Junior Football. Colin Bell was then approached to join Terry Farrell as the Director of Youth Football. Peter Swales resigned as Chairman as a result of much unrest from the supporters because of the continued lack of success. Francis Lee, who was the popular choice of the City 'Faithful', eventually took control. 'Forward With Franny' was the cry from an expectant following of 30.000 faithful supporters. Then Brian Horton was removed at the end of the 1994-95 season after City had finished 17th in the League.

With Francis Lee now firmly in control and eventually, amidst speculation and some disbelief from varying quarters. Alan Ball was brought in from Portsmouth to take over in 1995-96. I firmly believed that with the combination of Bell, on the Junior scene and Ball as First Team Manager we at last would achieve success. As players, Colin Bell and Alan Ball were top class. Francis Lee, although he'd been away from the game for sometime having great success with his business tradings and his Horse Racing as a trainer, I would have bet a Kings ransom that we now had a formula to lead us back to the top. Unfortunately, Alan just wasn't able to put together a side that could produce the goods and the shock of relegation was a major crisis that had to be faced with our Football now being in Division One. During season 1996-97 Alan was dismissed. Once more the search was on for a manager, or miracle worker!.

The ranks were not now producing to the extent they had done in the past. Luck alone wasn't enough. There were friction's that were very apparent and there was no one with the foresight to save the sinking ship. The Youth policy was very low, as was the first team, they were on a slide and no one from the Chairman, Peter Swales downwards, came forth with any direction or purpose to combat this downward trend.

This I would put down to instability and failure in management, which began to create a void in our Youth policy over the years. The supply and continued recruitment of young talent began to dwindle. There was no cohesion and a lack of management policies. Poorly made management appointments that proved very costly and ineffective. Panic began to set in and the rash managerial appointments that were made, hoping the unavoidable could be met to sustain further re-dress at our continued precarious league position. Steve Coppell gave it a try until - 'He wasn't well enough to cope!' Phil Neal tried to steady the boat, but he was 'up a creek without a paddle', just a pause in the 'manager go round'. Little or no discussions were held on Youth Football. Discussions regarding financial assistance, or policies concerning Youth development, were far and few between, particularly after Peter Reid and before Frank Clark.

During this period, about three years, there was never a single get together of Scouts, that there had been in the past, to discuss the policy of the Youth development at City. Whilst all around us, and I cite up the road at Manchester United plus, Liverpool, Leeds, Everton, Blackburn and many others. Progressive Directors and enterprising managers who had foreseen the future of the game and it's demands, cash wise, to either purchase top class highly priced players or, produce their own Youth lines by means of recruitment and, the building of a top class Youth Development Team to produce...

(a) A workable policy...

(b) The best men available to put the plan to use...

(c) The financial backing.

At Manchester United they put Brian Kidd and Nobby Stiles out to recruit the countries best kids. Eric Harrison to organise a sound coaching philosophy and the recruitment of the best available coaches. Likewise for Brian Kidd and Nobby Stiles with their Scouting network. Les Kershaw, with his ability to plan and organise. Paul McGuiness was added as Youth Team Administrator and here you have an established force second to none. The results at present date bear witness to this fact, that Alex Fergusons wisdom in backing a Youth policy, led to the wonderful climax of last season 1998-99, by winning three major trophies, which I feel will never be equaled.

Meanwhile, at Manchester City, we stood still and I, personally, was fraught and perturbed that we had dug a hole in which we might never climb out of. We had no one on board strong enough, or determined enough with a policy for City's recovery. The answer to all our problems arrived in a calamitous way, via our downward spiral of decay, with millions of pounds being spent to try and stave off the inevitable, but just a 'chink' of light appeared through one of the cracks. Then with us down near the relegation zone, Frank Clark was persuaded to take charge and it looked good that a man, with his pedigree, was to become manager. Amazingly, as much as any 100% City fan, will on reflection agree, though put down and castigated for his failure as a manager to stem the downward trend, Frank Clark did, on arrival, see

immediately the need to create action on City's Youth
Football set-up. It was in a sorry state and he ordered his
Assistant Manager Alan Hill, to undertake an immediate
review of the City Youth System and draw up a plan for
its revival as quickly as possible.

Frank and Alan put their proposals to new
Chairman Francis Lee; he willingly subscribed and put
their proposals to his Board members. It would be costly
in the initial stages, but changes were needed overnight.
Francis Lee was willing to back these initial changes,
unfortunately, they were made perhaps too rapidly and
caused some unpleasantness and people's services were
dispensed with. Neil McNab - Colin Bell and Terry
Farrell were given notice and this caused further unrest. I
think I would be right to say, or summarizing here, that
Frank Clark was 100% right in his judgment of the
situation he found upon his arrival. The Youth policy
was in a poor state, but surely, the blame lay on
mismanagement. Whoever had the role to manage wasn't
doing a good job. If there wasn't unity at the top of the
Youth Development, whose fault was it?

If Colin Bell and Terry Farrell's joint undertaking
as Youth Development Officers, and Neil McNab who
was Senior Coach to the Youth Team affairs, were not
cooperating with one another and causing an unstable
relationship. Then their immediate superior's i.e. the Club
Manager, or the Chief Scout, or whoever was responsible
for appraising their work and seeing that it was effective.
Were not fulfilling their role successfully and, should
have been removed and replaced by someone, who was
qualified with a vision and a policy to progress. The
sacking of the three seemed too drastic a measure.

We know Frank was under pressure, with the
continued decline of the first teams performances

obviously weighing on his mind. This may have had some effect on his decision. Frank Clark was a nice quiet easygoing man. I felt he lacked the personality and essential drive and ruthlessness to be effective. A manager must be firm and be seen to be in command. I felt he was just the opposite - quiet, kind and hopeful that his team, at management levels would eventually get things right. They patched up the squad with players of 'better days gone by', but paying very substantial fees for. Experienced players on whom he placed his faith, but not to be.

His decision to end Colin Bells and Neil McNab's association with City was a confounding issue, which he believed was correct. He felt that a friction existed between...

(a) The man (Colin Bell) who had the right to choose whom we signed on as Schoolboys.

(b) The man (Neil McNab) who was to coach them later at Youth level.

I admired both Colin and Neil as players. Colin needed no pats on the back, he was essentially a club man - gifted with ability - never cocky or brash - cool and reserved, he was one of City's best ever buys.

Colin was a typical 'Geordie', but he was never fond of the spotlight and shunned publicity. When injury ended his career as a footballer, he retired from any participation in the game and for a few years, he became a Restaurateur and was involved in one or two other business ventures as well. During this time he watched little or no football. Colin later sold his Restaurant and was persuaded to rejoin City in a dual role. Firstly, Scouting senior football for Jimmy Frizzell and later coaching the 'A' and 'B' sides. He also acted in a P.R.

capacity in meeting parents of prospective youngsters that City wanted to sign on.

Colin was kind and good-natured, but always honest in his handling of situations regarding youngsters, believing kindness was essential. If anything, he was perhaps to gentle in his nature. I enjoyed many occasions sitting with Colin and having a 'Cuppa' and chewing over and exchanging views on the game as it's played today. Colin is a sensible conversationalist who respected other people's points of view.

One player, who Colin and I both thought would be a good investment, was Dean Windass. Dean was a strong left-sided player, playing at Hull City at the time. We made him out as the best player in the lower Division soccer and we both agreed he would be the ideal replacement for Peter Beagrie. I actually rated him better than Beagrie as he could win the ball - be constructive - defend and support the strikers, an honest 100% player. Hull City wanted £500.000, Jimmy Frizzell said we had no cash, so Aberdeen paid £450.000 for him. He is at present playing for Bradford City in the Premiership, I might add here, alongside Peter Beagrie.

Neil McNab was a volatile Scottish International who joined Arsenal as a youngster, later moved on and eventually arrived at Manchester City, where he soon established his popularity, with his no nonsense approach as a ball winner in his mid-field role. He left City after a successful spell and finally ended his career at Tranmere Rovers.

The first contact I had with Neil after he left City was when I approached him during a Reddish Junior League game about his twin sons Joe and Neil Jnr. They were playing for a Denton side at U-10/11 and I obviously wanted to make our interest in them known.

Neil was still playing with Tranmere and I asked if he would let us have a look at them at City. He initially declined because he thought it too early, but eventually they did join us when Neil accepted a post as Youth Team Coach with City.

I gained his respect immediately as my Protégé Lee Crooks had taken Neil's eye and he complimented me on my selection, he was sure that Lee would make the grade. Neil and I got along very well and we often chatted and he respected my views on the game in general. Colin and Neil were as different as blue and green!.

I remember one occasion when the Youth team was playing Hereford in the F.A. Youth Cup Quarter Final. I was talking with the lads in general and asked their opinions of Colin and Neil. They respected and admired both of them, but felt that Colin was too gentle and would always cajole them, whereas Neil demanded, perhaps bullied at times, but treated everyone the same, including his own two boys. Neil would expect that you did things his way and he was never satisfied until you did. He turned boys into men, they said. I was personally upset and disappointed when Frank Clark severed their connections with City.

Whilst promotion was the prime objective, plans were laid to fund a massive effort to establish an Academy of Soccer that would be the envy of all our competitors. With this aim underway, sadly, our troubles with the first team performances were not solved and with further crises looming and Frank Clark unable to achieve satisfactory results, he decided to resign adding further gloom for the Chairman and all concerned with Manchester City. But a ray of sunshine was emerging. Francis Lee had seen the necessity to continue his support

for funding an up todate Youth Policy and Before Frank
Clark resigned, he recruited Jim Cassell from Oldham
Athletic to become the head of Manchester City's New
Youth Academy.

Good fortune, but costly as Frank Clark's sacking
of the three was. It allowed Alan Hill, Frank's assistant,
the opportunity to immediately set to work to right the
situation. He did this, as I said, by approaching Jim
Cassell, who was at the time, Youth Development Officer
at Oldham Athletic, to come and discuss with him and
Frank Clark the possibility of taking over City's Youth
Development Program. This was accomplished with the
blessing of Francis Lee and his Board of Directors. The
outcome, and to you who bayed for Frank Clark's blood,
can thank your lucky stars, that Jim Cassell was
persuaded, to join City as it's head of Youth
Development, with assurances of a free reign and
financial backing to introduce a successful Youth Policy.
In Jim's words...

"It will take about five years to flourish".
He said he would make it work if given the financial
backing.

Very painstakingly, Jim planned the Youth Policy,
but Francis Lee succumbed to mounting pressure and
resigned the Chairmanship of City, he handed over to
David Bernstein and, they both were in agreement in
giving Jim Cassell, 100% backing in his policy and
decisions. Odd decisions in change, and sometimes
objected to, but overall, in just three years he attained a
success undreamed of and our Youth Policy at
Manchester City is second to none. It is a very privileged
young man who today is invited to come and try his luck
with us. Today we no longer have to pick up the
remnants, choice is ours now, as our standard of boy,

playing with pride in City colours, from the age of 9 - 19 years, is second to none.

Even though the club was immersed in deeper problems of further relegation at Pro-Level, the emergence of this wonderful venture began. It is successful beyond belief. A vast fortune has been spent on the development of City's training complex at Platt Lane, to such an extent, that it is has become one of the finest in the Country. We will, I believe in five years or thereabouts, reap the benefits of this wonderful venture, mainly due to the efforts of Francis Lee and current Chairman, David Bernstein and his hard working fellow Directors.

I hope this will give all our wonderful supporters great hope, that we are shortly to produce once again, a few Paul Lakes and the like, who will once again take us on to past glories and achieve for you, the supporters, honours you so richly deserve. I feel that it won't be long until we attain our rightful place among the higher echelon. To see the names of Manchester City players displayed in all the International lineups, be it English, Irish, Scottish or Welsh.

From tragedy and chaos, you should thank Frank Clark and his Assistant Alan Hill, for their foresight. Francis Lee and his Board for their backing. To current Chairman Davis Bernstein and his Board for their continued backing and promise of further help. Joe Royle and his Assistant Willie Donechie, who have put the first team on an even keel and I'm sure, quite capable of reaching greater heights. We have weathered the storm well so far. Let us hope that when Eastlands opens its doors, we can recapture some of this great clubs past glories.

Joe Royle was eventually persuaded to take control, albeit late in the day, and after a valiant effort we were relegated into Division two for the first time in the clubs history. It was good to see a side battling with a pride and distinction for some 30.000 supporters who deserve nothing less than to see this Club back at the top where it belongs. Joe Royle and Willie Donechie were working hard to turn things around, and we held a remote chance of making the play-offs and hopefully promotion back to Division One.

Our Academy is up and running so smoothly under the guidance of Jim Cassell. Jim brought in Barry Poynton, as Recruitment Officer for Youth Development, along with Alex Gibson 'Ex Lillieshall Chief Coach' as Director of Youth Coaching. Under their guidance, boys from the ages of seven to sixteen plus our under-17 and under-19 Academy sides, all being coached at our wonderful facility at Platt Lane Manchester. It is also at Platt Lane on Sunday mornings where Jimmy Fox along with Eric Mullender who administer our new recruits coming in for coaching from the age of seven.

Thanks to all our supporters who subscribe in any way, large or small, towards helping us achieve our goal. The Facility is there for all to see on any Sunday morning and during our mid-week coaching evenings, for you to come along and feel proud of what your contributions are bringing to Manchester City's Theatre of Dreams

Ken Barnes

"The best un-capped wing half I've ever seen"

Steve Fleet

"Steve developed a great Youth side for Manchester City
in 1978/79 winning the Lancashire Youth Cup. Steve was
until recently, Manager of the Manchester City Complex
at Platt Lane. He was ultimately responsible for its
everyday running for both Manchester City and its very
successful Community work in conjunction with the
Local City Council. He was ably assisted by Gary Walker,
Phil Eddleston and Ralph Innes"

Chapter 6

"A Few Good Prospects"

Scouting isn't always as straightforward as it seems to be. I always try to arrive as early as I can wether it is a schoolboy game or a Pro-Game. Getting there prior to kick-off is essential, especially in obtaining whatever local information on schoolboy prospects, or the Pro, that you can. The spectator's view can be invaluable.

Trying to obtain information can be difficult at the best of times. Making an approach must be done in the correct manor. Sometimes having made your approach the man in charge, a Schoolteacher or the Sunday team manager can be a little difficult and refuse to help. Why they are is beyond me. I think perhaps it is a little selfish on their part. The choice when all is said and done is surely down to the boy and his parents. It is a chance for some youngster to have the opportunity of making a career for himself and what can be wrong in that. Having met with these obstacles the Scout may, although only rarely, resort to other means of getting the information he needs. Getting information on Schoolboys from the Liverpool and Stoke areas was virtually impossible in the early days, unless you were from their particular part of the World. I have on many an occasion given some youngster two 'bob' to go and ask the number eleven for his name and phone number, if he had one that is. I also remember having to literally go into the showers to get someone's name because; the team manager refused point blank to give me the information. On the whole though, presenting yourself in the proper manor and displaying your representative pass is all that is required. Most Schoolteachers and club managers are very helpful and co-operative.

When at Leeds I found myself more or less restricted to within a 30 - 90 mile territory. Now at Manchester City and with my new unrestrained freedom I could now roam into Derbyshire - Yorkshire and the Midlands to cover Schoolboy football and the odd Pro-Match. I would do a schoolboy game in the morning and a Pro-Match in the afternoon. I also took in some Sunday games covering all the age groups.

One of my first junior finds was on Ashton Moss in 1976 watching a team called Waterloo. I was very impressed with an eleven-year-old defender by the name of Michael Queenan. Although playing with an older age group he showed a lot of tenacity and toughness along with his natural skill.

I thought - 'He looks like one for the future'.

I then contacted his father Terry. Terry was an ex-player himself and I expressed our interest in his lad and said that I thought he was one for the future. The boy progressed well and went on to play for the Oldham Boys Town Team, the Manchester County Team and finally the England Schoolboys in 1980 - of course during this time Manchester City signed him on schoolboy-forms and upon leaving school he joined City as an apprentice. Unfortunately he never made it to the Pro-Ranks. It's difficult to say where he failed, but not all prospects make the grade. Andy Ritchie, now manager of Oldham Athletic, was one of many I had the good fortune to pass on as a good prospect that did go on to have a successful career.

Andy Ritchie trained with Manchester City as a schoolboy up to the age of thirteen. He couldn't commit

himself to any club at that time because he went to
Moseley Hall Grammar School Stockport and the school
demanded all his services, usually on Saturday mornings
for rugby or cross country running. It was only after
pressure from his dad Jim that he was allowed to play for
Stockport Boys Town Team Under-14's.

Prior to my coming to City and whilst I was still at
Leeds I invited Andy to visit and play in trials at Elland
Road. I then moved to Manchester City and one of my
first duties was to recommend both Ray Ranson and
Andy to Ken Barnes. Ken said that Andy was already
training at City and he felt certain that Andy would sign.
I knew that his dad Jim was letting the lad have a look at
other clubs before making up his mind. I pointed this out
to Ken, at this point in time, as I stated earlier, boys
weren't signed until their fourteenth birthday. This
allowed the more fashionable and richer clubs to bide
their time and move in at the last moment. This wouldn't
be allowed to happen today because of the safeguards of
Academy and School of Excellence contracts that boys
now have to sign from the age of nine. Andy eventually
signed for Manchester United at fourteen.

This caused Ken a little embarrassment and his
faith and belief were shattered as he had kept on good
terms with Andy's dad Jim. There is no worse a feeling
than having done all the groundwork and time spent in
getting a prospect to your club and then lose him at the
eleventh hour to the opposition. Ray Ranson on the
otherhand did sign for us.

I first saw **Ray Ranson** play for St.Helens Boys
whilst I was still at Leeds and I recommended that we
should have him in for trials, but once again no one
seemed interested.   I thought he was good enough to
make the England Boys trial, which he eventually did.

A lot of other clubs began to show an interest in him. Now that I was at City, I managed to talk Ken Barnes and Director Freddy Pye into going to see Ray's parents and try to use their influence in getting his signature, not that Ray needed much persuading, he was 'Man City Daft'.

Ken and Freddy went over to Liverpool to see and entertain Ray's parents. They invited them to a lavish meal at Liverpool's Adelphi Hotel, which was a little more than they were accustomed to, I felt this would be ideal, we always did it at Leeds, and it was a nice touch. The evening went well, and we won them over. The following day, Freddy said to me...

"I hope your right about this lad Davies, he's cost me an arm and leg so far, I had to put them all up for the night as well, at the Adelphi".

I then tried a little 'con' on Freddy, I talked him into a 'free' Airline ticket to Sydney Australia and back, when and if Ray makes his first team debut, that's how convinced I was of his ability. When Ray finally did, Freddy Pye had a convenient lapse of memory.

Other clubs, that were showing an interest were indecisive in coming to a decision and ultimately when Ray came to have a look at us, he said he liked it here and would accept the apprenticeship we offered. Ray went on to play nine times for England Schoolboys, seven times for the England Youth Team and eventually won ten full International Caps. He also played 181 games for the Manchester City first team. He came back on loan to City in January 1993 and played a further 18 games. I was over the moon to say the least. Ray always keeps in touch, and always seeks me out for a chat whenever he comes to Maine Road. He's always been appreciative of my faith in him and my conduct towards his parents.

I had no problems either with my next recommendation. I went to watch a game at Abbey Hey Football Club. I had gone in particular to view a boy who didn't come up to scratch. It was a game in the Reddish League Sunday Cup and my eye was drawn to a lively winger wearing the number seven shirt for Haddon Hall F.C. His name was **Dave Bennett**. I thought I should have another closer look at him as I thought he looked a good prospect, he was far above Sunday League standard.

I went to see him play in an arranged game and immediately got in touch with the Haddon Hall officials to make an approach to Dave and his dad. I eventually got together with Dave and his dad and they were pleasantly surprised when I asked if Dave would like to come along for coaching and training with Steve Fleet who was our Youth Team coach at that time. Mr. Bennett also thought that I should be having a look at Dave's younger brother Garry. Mr. Bennett thought that Garry was a better prospect.

I brought **Garry Bennett** in a little later after Dave had signed on for us. Steve was over the moon with Garry who could play either centre-half or centre forward, he made him kingpin of the defence and everyone knows just what a good prospect he turned out to be. Garry is currently with Darlington and still turning out good performances at the age of 37.

Dave eventually turned professional and did very well for City playing 43 first team games but lost favour and was eventually sold for the meagre sum of £100.000 along with his brother Gary, who for some unknown reason, was allowed to go on a 'free' to Cardiff City. Dave was then sold on to Coventry and Garry to Sunderland at considerably bigger fees and wages. We of course had no sell on clause - so Sunderland and Cardiff did well.

Nicky Reid was one of the nicest kids I ever met in junior football. I found him at the age of ten. Again whilst I was still at Leeds I took him to play for Pudsey Juniors who were, in essence Leeds nursery side. This was an under-12 side and easily the best in Yorkshire at that time. Nicky was quiet as a mouse off the field, but he was a terror on it, he hated to lose no matter how big or good his opponent was Nicky played to win. He may have lacked a little finesse, but always gave 110%. Although he was a little younger than Andy Ritchie or Dave Bennett, I told Ken that I'd had him down at Leeds a couple of times, and being that we had him training at City I felt that we should sign him as soon as possible. I know that if I had stayed at Leeds he would have definitely signed for them.

Nicky was a terrific young lad and was always courteous to my wife Lil and me. Whenever we met him at some junior function or presentation he would always address us as 'Mr. & Mrs.Davies'. He said It was his mark of respect for the help I had given to him. He was a tremendous professional and would play anywhere he was told. He was sold to the Seattle Sounders (USA) in May 1982, there were cries of nepotism as John Bonds son John Jr. replaced him.

Nicky only lasted a short time in America and he returned home to City. Nicky was just beginning to mature at City and did his job well, now playing in mid-field. He played a total of 211 games for City before being let go on a 'free' to Blackburn Rovers in July 1987. He is now player Manager at Sligo Rovers at this point in time 1999. One of my favourite players, he is a lad I will always admire and have respect for.

Steve Kinsey, who now resides in the USA where he coaches the Florida Thundercats, was another product of our junior side Whitehill Juniors. I felt that we should sign Steve and I persuaded Ken Barnes to take him on.

Steve was only slight in build, but had good skill with a desire and an honesty to do well and with an eye for scoring goals. I felt he would mature to a good standard. He signed Pro' forms in May 1979.

He was loaned out early in his career to Chester and later to Chesterfield. Steve made progress and eventually made it into the first team where he played 87 times before being sold to the Minnesota Strikers for £25.000 in October 1986. He played for various clubs throughout the next 12 years eventually ending up in Florida. Unfortunately for Steve nature hadn't been to kind and his slight build wasn't tough enough for the rigors of top class football. Steve was able to adjust to the U.S. standard of play - which at that time concentrated on the indoor circuit. Steve has settled into the American way of life and now teaches youngsters as well as participating occasionally.

Clive Wilson was another bit of good luck that you have from time to time. It was on a Wednesday evening in 1977. I had gone to the Manchester County F.A. Grounds to view a lad who had been recommended and didn't turn out to be anything special. There were two games being played that evening on adjoining pitches. Not being interested in the boy I had come to view I decided to watch a little of the game on the other pitch. I became intrigued with this small left footer playing for Hulme Lads Club. He had a great left foot and marvellous skills that were far better than anyone we had in the junior ranks. I was mesmerised by his nice touch and skill.

Immediately the game ended I made straight for him and asked if he would care to come along and meet Steve Fleet the following evening. I asked him if he could come along with 'Big' Alex William's, who had just commenced training with us. Clive and Alex both shared the same birthdate - November 13th.1961. Alex was a tremendous Goalkeeping prospect, such was his ability that he went on to become City's first choice keeper in 1982 keeping out the great Joe Corrigan, his career was cut short through a back injury. Clive agreed to this and Steve Fleet was in Raptures and was convinced that he could groom this boy into becoming a top professional.

Clive continued to progress until he was about 19 or 20 years old. He then began to feel he had gone as far as he could. He was playing regularly for the reserves and performing well, but unable to break into the first team. He became a little despondent and was loaned out twice to Chester in September and again in November 1982. He began to feel really down and he spoke to me of giving up soccer and going back to his studies. I managed to talk him out of this idea and work even harder and recognition would come. Then his break came.
City was in the old Second Division at that time and were leaving Friday night to play Wolves. I found out that Clive would be playing. I rang his Mam and Dad to tell him and to wish him all the best. Not only did he play, but also the local Sunday Paper raved over his performance and gave him a rating of ten. His career was now underway and his game began to blossom. He went on to be a good professional for City playing a total of 107 times. Eventually Chelsea came in with a bid of £500.000 for him. He won a Championship medal with them in 1989 and even today at the age of 37 he is still playing the odd game for Tottenham. He is at present doing his bit

for Cambridge United. I take my hat off to him and I think he is still a joy to watch.

It is in all probability that Clive would have been picked up by some other Scout because he was such a good player. There must be hundreds of kids who are out there playing and displaying equal amounts of skill and never getting an opportunity. It's being in the right game at the right time. Hoping that someone will spot them and give them the same kind of chance to fulfill their dreams.

Earl Barratt is as nice and pleasant a lad now as he was the day I first met him. I'd received a request from his club Royton Youth asking for a trial.

Off I went one rainy Sunday afternoon to have a look. He was a tall rangy type of player and I was impressed the moment I saw him. He was playing right back for the first time, but I didn't know this at the time. I asked his coach if I might have a chat with his right back. He was more than pleased and introduced me to a very puzzled and perplexed Earl Barratt.

Earl was a Rochdale schoolboy who only got the odd game for his school team. Also surprisingly he was not even considered good enough for the town team under-15 eleven, someone must have been asleep on this selection committee. I asked if he would like to come to City and take part in some training and coaching.

Steve Fleet eventually gave Earl a game for the 'B' team against Glasgow Celtic Juniors who were on a visit to Manchester. After a nervous start, Earl went on to have a good game and came through with flying colours. Earl was still attending school at this time and played in 4 more games for City before the season came to a close. They decided that if Earl measured up in his last game before the end of season, it was a game on the

Wednesday afternoon May 7th against Everton's Youth Team that had just won the Youth Cup, he would be offered an apprenticeship.

This was marvelous news for him, but he was also due to sit his G.C.E. exam that same day. This was an obvious problem - contact was then made with his Headmaster who simply asked...
"If Earl is successful! What then?"
We said he would be granted an apprenticeship, the Headmaster granted him a stay of execution regarding his exams. Earl played out of his skin and won his apprenticeship.

Earl eventually made the pro-ranks but again someone at management levels decided to release Earl and he signed for Oldham for £23.000. He made tremendous progress and Oldham eventually sold him for £1.700.000 to Aston Villa. Earl, believe it or not, was reluctant to go. He listened to a lot of good advice telling him that he would be foolish not to go, he then accepted, getting a higher pay packet and his cut of the transfer fee never really bothered him as he was happy and contented where he was. But off to Aston Villa he went.

I would like to add that prior to him moving to Villa, Earl was selected to join the England squad in Australia due to an injury to one of the defenders, Earl was flown out to join up with the rest of the team. Having a couple of hours to spare whilst waiting to change planes at Sydney Airport Earl phoned me to tell me where he was. My wife Lil answered the phone and he explained who he was and asked for me, she told him I was at Maine Road and could she take a message. He only had a few minutes to spare as he was at the Airport in Sydney waiting for his flight to join up with the England squad. Earl added that he just wanted to phone me because I was the one who had made it all possible and he wanted to say thank you.

Whilst he was over there he was interviewed by a World Wide Soccer Magazine and he reiterated, when asked by his interviewer, who he felt he owed his good fortune to, he said...

"A chubby little football Scout named Len Davies at Manchester City who came out to watch a bunch of kids play on a wet Sunday afternoon in Royton Lancashire".

Earl is now retired from playing and pursuing a new career in coaching.

I've obviously had lads who made the grade, some, who stayed, some who moved on. I think that no matter at what level they play, I think I have earned their respect. Lads like Chris Lucketti who is now at Huddersfield and Andy Thackery, still plodding on at Halifax, two smashing lads who are still courteous enough to find me a few minutes for a chat. These are treasures you can't buy. There are others, but I just bring these two to mind who are still enjoying their football.

I first spotted **Chris Lucketti** playing for Senrab - (Whitehill Juniors). He was playing in a side of 12 and 13 year olds against an Under-15 side from Hollingworth near Manchester, although they were giving plenty away in age and size, Chris's side showed a lot of determination and spirit in earning a very good 5-5 draw. This was just prior to the new season 1984.

Chris was about 13 years old and played as a striker. He had good vision and strong with terrific balance. I made it my business to introduce myself to his parents and get his particulars. Chris is a Rochdale lad and his parents still live in the same area. I told Ken Barnes that here was another good prospect. At this point in time, we did our training and held our trials at the facility we had hired from the Cheadle Council, but unfortunately, the lease was not renewed. Barry Bennall, who was responsible for the trials and training, acquired permission from Crewe Alexandra to use their training facilities.

Bennall was seeking a full time coaching position at City, but was refused. He then took a part-time job on the Youth Development side with Crewe and consequently took all the Senrab boys, including Chris with him. Chris didn't commit himself to Crewe and he continued to look around the Lancashire Clubs until Rochdale offered him an apprenticeship in 1987. From there, Chris then went to Stockport, Halifax , Bury and at present with Huddersfield. Upto press, I believe one or two clubs are looking at the possibility of obtaining his services. Wherever he ends up playing, I wish him and his family all the very best, he is, in my estimation, a polite winner. My earlier judgment proving me correct.

Andy Thackerey was a lad I saw just once and I was convinced I'd seen enough. He was playing for Huddersfield Boys in September 1981 playing against Tameside.

Good fortune favoured me on this fixture in that, I followed my normal routine, in checking with the home team secretary, early in the week, to ensure the game would still be on and where it would be played. As luck would have it, Alan Millea the secretary of Tameside informed me that, the under-14 and under-15 matches would be played Friday night, with a 5.30pm K.O. and not on the usual Saturday.

I set off straight from work on the Friday, and upon my arrival, I began to watch the under-15 game. The standard wasn't up to much, and the only boy with any ability was already signed to a Pro' Club. I then concentrated on the under-14 game and this tall and stylish right-winger caught my attention. The boy had a lovely first touch - good control - two footed and decent pace, he also had a reasonably accurate shot, stronger with his right. An outstanding prospect I thought.

My luck was in, no other Scouts were there, unaware of the fixture switch. His dad was on hand, assisting the Tameside manager. I had a long conversation with Andy's dad, who told me that Andy was training at Huddersfield once a week, but so far hadn't signed anything with them. His dad accepted my invitation to bring Andy to City for a trial, this he did successfully and Andy was signed on Schoolboy Forms.

Andy joined at about the same time as David White, he and Andy became very close friends. Andy progressed very well and was a part of our successful Youth side that beat the old enemy from Old Trafford on April 29th 1986 2-0 in front of 18.000 spectators at Maine Road. Incidentally, Andy was sent off in the first leg at Old Trafford after a confrontation with Uniteds Murphy.

Our Team at Maine Road on that April night was...
Crompton - Mills - Hinchcliffe - Brightwell - Redmond - Thackerey - White - Moulden - Lake - Scott and Boyd.

Unfortunately, the Manager thought that Andy wasn't up to standard for the first team, and they released him at the end of that season 1986. This didn't deter Andy, and he has gone on to play over 500 games in his professional career at Huddersfield / Newport / Wrexham / Rochdale and still playing today with Halifax.

Sensibly, Andy has maintained a high standard of fitness and an understanding that, life goes on. Along with his football career, Andy has worked hard and qualified as a Chiropodist and when his football career is finally over, he will hopefully be able to embark on his new career.

Another Andy I spotted was **Andy Elliott**, a local Glossop lad. Andy became part of Steve Fleets successful Lancashire Youth Cup winning side in 1978/79. I had brought in six of those boys, Andy, Steve Kinsey, Garry Bennett, Clive Wilson, Geoff Lomax, who is now an Academy coach at City and Gary Fitzgerald.

I first spotted Andy in 1976 playing for his local Glossop School team and I got him a game playing for Hillgate Juniors of Ashton, he was twelve years old. He played in mid-field and his biggest asset was his passion and desire, he hated losing. He was nominated at 13/14 for trials for Northwest Derbyshire and then for Derbyshire Boys. It was at this point I brought him to City and under Steve Fleet's guidance he was invited for trials for England Boys, but his lack of inches was his undoing and he wasn't selected. However, he signed Schoolboy forms for City and eventually got an apprenticeship followed by a Pro contract and a regular place in Dave Ewings Reserve side. This eventually led to a first team debut against Middlesboro' at nineteen years old. He got two more chances, but again, nature wasn't too kind to him, although gutsy and tenacious, his lack of pace let him down and he was eventually released. He went on to play successfully for Sligo Rovers and then Chester City and Rochdale. Andy is now currently pursuing a career in coaching and is currently taking his F.A. Licence with the Manchester County F.A. and awaiting his final assessment. Andy is happily married to wife Gill and is still living locally in Hadfield where I am keeping an eye on his eight-year old son Alex, who looks a likely prospect.

There is a lot of luck in Scouting in that, you go to view someone in particular and end up finding something better by pure chance. This has happened to me before on a couple of occasions. This particular time was when I went with a Scouting compatriot of mine named Trevor Gee, who was just beginning as a Scout. We went one Sunday afternoon to watch an under-14 Junior Cup Match near Frickley Colliery. We arrived at about 1.30pm for a 2.00pm K.O..

Whilst we were waiting we started watching an under-12 game that was already in progress. I became absorbed with this 'blondish haired' mid-field player who had a good physique for his age. He ran the game with good controlled long passes and a strong and accurate shot. I asked Trevor to watch the under-14 game and make notes of anyone that stood out, I continued to watch the under-12 game and I said I would catch up with him in awhile. He came back saying that there was nothing outstanding on view.

I decided to try my luck and see what I could find out about the 'blond haired' youngster. As luck would have it, his father Terry, was manager - coach and linesman too. I trotted up and down the line gathering information on the boy, his name was **Lee Crooks**.

I invited Terry to bring Lee down to Manchester on the following Tuesday, this he did and he then continued every Tuesday and Thursday. During this time he also managed to pay a visit to Oldham Athletic whilst Joe Royle was manager there. Lee then decided when he was fifteen years old to join Manchester City.

He attended England Schoolboy trials and represented England at Under-15/16 and 17. He maintained a steady progress under Neil McNab's watchful eye and eventually made the first team at 18 years of age. On his debut in the first team, he suffered an injury to his foot playing against Middlesboro', thus creating a slight setback. Lee recovered and his reward is at this point in time, regular first team duties under Joe Royle and Willie Donechie's guidance, albeit now at right fullback. He recently scored his first goal for City and what a goal it was!. It was a scorcher against Chesterfield, and the first of many we hope!.

I've had a lot of success in the past with my recommendations to City. Quite a few who have gone on to make the first team and have successful careers, others who have gone on to be successful at other clubs after leaving City. Being able to provide a youngster with the opportunity of having a career in doing something he enjoys, is the most pleasing aspect of being a Scout. Even in the twilight of my Scouting career I'm still able to find the odd prospect, as in Lee Crooks. I also hope that my current recommendations will provide a star or two for the future. Prospects like young Terry Dunfield. He has just signed a Professional Contract for City in April 1999 and won his first England U-17 Cap, he is also going with the England Under-17 Squad to Spain in January 2000.

Terry Dunfield arrived at City for trials as an under thirteen from Vancouver in British Columbia, Canada in 1995. He came with a group of boys brought over by Ted McDougal, the Ex-Manchester United and Southampton player who is Coach for the Development of Youth Football in British Columbia, Canada.

Alan Ball, who was the current Manager of City at the time and Chairman Francis Lee, asked me if I would observe and write reports on any outstanding prospects from within the group.

I would report to them and Ted McDougal as to any boy I thought might be worth having back for further observation. I said that there were possibly 3 or 4, but there was one who I thought showed maturity and class. When Alan and Francis asked me for my assessment of him I said that, if he were a local Manchester lad he would make the Town Team levels and possibly County grade also.

Francis Lee held discussions with Terry's parents in possibly allowing Terry to spend his last two years of Schooling here in Manchester. This would allow him to, not only train, but play in our Under-14 team. This seemed acceptable to Terry's Dad as they had family connections in Prestbury Manchester.

Terry's Mother was very supportive and agreed to move to England with him. She then decided on renting a home and bringing Terry's brother Ryan, who is a very capable footballer in his own right to join them and go to School with Terry in Macclesfield. This would be better than having to commute periodically from Canada. Terry's Dad stayed in Canada and joined them as often has he could, being self employed this presented no problem to him.

Terry has progressed very rapidly and as I stated earlier, has just signed Pro-Forms with City. It's early days yet to predict just how far his career will develop, but he is only a young man and with the right encouragement and guidance, who knows what the future holds. As I write, Terry has just been awarded his first England U-17 Cap. I sincerely hope that my advice given to Terry and his parents, Kim and Sharon bears fruit. They have given up so much for him in order for him to attain his goal. I know he appreciates what they have done for him, also all those who have encouraged and helped him on his way.

Another youngster I recently recommended, that City have high hopes for is, Nadum Onouhda. Nadum is now approaching thirteen years old and of Nigerian Parents.

I first spotted him playing for Clayton Juniors, Manchester in a six-a-side under-10 competition. What caught my eye was his speed. This is emphasised by his prowess as an Athlete at School. He is a pupil at William Hulme Grammar School, Manchester where he excels in Athletic Field Events. He recently won 4 Gold Medals at County Level in several of these events. He also took part in the 1999 National Schools Athletic Championships at Birmingham where he came first in the Hop-Step and Jump. He lost out in the sprint events due to a groin strain, which has curtailed both his Athletics and Football for this season.

Nadum can play Football in various positions and as yet is undecided as to his best spot. We again must thank both Parents, Martin and Antonia for supporting Nadum and staying on here in the U.K. where they have studied for their Degrees at Salford University, also raising four children aged 2/8/12 and 14. Incidentally, Antonia is continuing to study at Liverpool for her Doctorate in Science. Well done to both of them, now it's up to you Nadum.

Only time will tell wether Terry and Nadum succeed or not. I, being on my `Last Lap' so to speak, feel that our Youth Development will be a success and begin to produce talent comparable to the likes of Paul Lake etc.

I feel confident in that it will achieve this and restore this Club to its former glories.

Andy Ritchie

"One for the future, I thought"

Ray Ranson

"Ray was Man City daft"

Dave Bennett

"An F.A. Cup winner with Coventry"

Garry Bennett

"A good Pro' still plying his trade in 2000"

Steve Kinsey

"Steve had plenty of heart"

Nicky Reid

"Always gave 110%"

Clive Wilson

"A great left foot"

Alex Williams

"City's number one keeper in 1982"

Colin Bell

"Starred for City from 1965-78"

**Frankie Bunn – Paul Power – Alex Gibson
Barry Poynton – Jim Cassell**

"Youth Development Team"

Joe Royle

"Joe Royle, in his playing day's at City"

Joe Royle

"Back in the Premiership!
We've been kissed by Lady Luck!
But after what this Club has been through in the past,
we deserve it"

Chapter 7

"Some That Got Away"

In 1975/76 Gary Birtles was playing for Long Eaton United in the Midland League. Two acquaintances of mine, one with a league club and the other on the committee of the Midland League, suggested I should have a look at this outstanding prospect who was about nineteen at the time.

I passed this information on to Ken Barnes who said that, rather than I travel to the Midlands to view him, he would ask a relative of his, who was an 'ex-player' and living in the area, to go and do the assessment, a common-sense of 'economics'.

Kens relative got in touch and said that he had been to see the lad and suggested that we make contact as soon as possible. He added that, the lad was everything that had been said about him, and that he was the best prospect and best non-league player he had seen. Ken followed up by watching Birtles himself and agreed with everyone. It was then suggested that Ken and I would go to long Eaton and make any move we felt necessary to induce the lad to come to Maine Road for a month's trial. This was to be the following Saturday.

Ken asked me what sort money did I think would be involved in getting the lad. He wanted to know what I thought the initial outlay for loss of earnings and what sort of money would Long Eaton be looking for, also what the lad would be looking for personally. I said perhaps about £100-150 a week for loss of earnings and about £20.000 - £30.000 for his transfer.

The Saturday we should have gone to Long Eaton Ken had a domestic problem and we couldn't get there.

On the following Monday I phoned Ken to say that my contact in the Midlands had been in touch, and it looked as if we had missed the boat as Nottingham Forest had stepped in. Brian Clough had been to see Gary play for Long Eaton against Enderby, with a view to taking the lad on. When 'Cloughy' was asked what his opinion of Gary was, he was reported to have said...

"The half-time Oxo was more impressive!".

He nonetheless must have seen something he liked, because they signed him.

This was unfortunate on our part. Ken said he would not have been permitted to meet personal terms and Long Eatons transfer figure, without first discussing it with the board.   Forest gave the lad £50.00 a week initially and paid his Club £2000.00. We would have gone as far as £150.00 per week and £10.000 - £20.000 to the Club. Nottingham Forest had been informed of other clubs interests and acted, they gambled on the belief that he would be a winner - and the rest you know.

Another who got away, albeit temporarily. A friend of mine Charlie Fletcher at Sheffield Wednesday phoned me and advised me to run the rule over a twenty-year old lad named Kevin Reeves who was with Bournemouth and who were managed by 'ex' City Manager and player John Benson.

Charlie had recommended him to Sheffield Wednesday, who were quoted £50.000, but funds were unfortunately not available at the time. Respecting Charlie's judgment I mentioned this to Ken, thinking perhaps he could pull the 'old acquaintance' act and gain a step on other interested clubs. John Benson said that Norwich were favourites to land him but were having difficulties in raising the money. We again didn't bother, it would have meant going to the board again and by that time, the 'bus' would have gone.

It's amazing that just a couple of years later we paid Norwich over a million pounds for him. I'm lost for words, or perhaps I should say words not mentionable. When things like this happened, I often wondered...

"What's the point in raising these issues?".

These are honest bits of Scouting that I think are worth mentioning. I don't want to sound like I'm grumbling, but I suppose I am...

...I just want to show how lacking a Chairman and his board were at times, in limiting the power of attorney to those whom they have appointed to get the best possible prospects for the club. If Chief Scouts, who have their hands tied whilst being employed by boastful egotists, who have proved nothing in years of management and who have squandered millions in attaining nothing!...

"Then what is the point?".

I don't think I need to mention names.

Ken Barnes, if given the freedom to move without restraints, could have and would have attained both Gary Birtles and Kevin Reeves for less than a £100.000. Ken wont squawk, being the good professional that he is. He just accepted his position and took the good with the bad.

Paul Heaton who went on to become an established 'pro' at Oldham was another who I felt got away from us at City. Nature unfortunately wasn't too kind to him as a schoolboy. He was a rather skinny lad, but I; nonetheless, felt he had what it takes to become a professional footballer.

Paul had a will and honesty, along with his determination and skill that suggested to me that he would make the grade. Consequently I took him along to Maine Road during his last year at school. He trained

Tuesday and Thursday evenings with our part timers. Unfortunately our staff coaches and trainers thought he didn't have the physical attributes needed to be a top professional and turned him down. This they did without him ever being subjected to a full trial, in a game of his own age group, or in a team of City juniors against similar opposition.

This didn't deter Paul and he wrote to Oldham asking for a trial. He was invited along and from there, he showed Jimmy Frizzell, who was Oldham's manager at the time, that he had enough to be offered an apprenticeship and eventually being signed as a full time professional.

Physically he may not have looked the perfect specimen, but along with his skill and determination and a willingness to play anywhere and at any time he showed what a good professional he was. I watched him play at School, 8 games or more a week, never in the same position twice and never with a complaint, just as long as he got a game, he got on with it. At weekends he would often play Saturday and Sunday mornings and afternoons. Funny as it may seem - City and many other clubs watched and admired and considered whether they should make a bid for him, City had contemplated making a £400.000 bid, after turning him down initially.

Any youngster with a belief in his own ability, should not be deterred by others inability to spot potential. It is a human trait to err and make mistakes sometimes. Just fight your initial disappointment and try to prove to yourself and to others that you have what it takes. The self-satisfaction if you do succeed is pleasure money can't buy. Paul never held it against me because City didn't keep him on and whenever we meet, he always has time for a chat and I always get a card at Christmas, these are my personal pleasures.

About the same time I had another youngster who we let slip away, **Darren McDonough**. I spotted Darren playing for Failsworth Juniors at U-11. He joined our Junior side Whitehill. He wasn't a classic player, he lacked a bit of precision in his delivery, but he always gave 110%, he was very strong and honest as they come. He wasn't favoured to make it and we let him go at U-13-14. He went on to complete an apprenticeship and signed Pro-Forms, again with Oldham Athletic. He was later sold to Luton Town who paid £300.000 for him. City, again even contemplated making a bid for him as we were struggling a bit with our defense. Rumours had it that he wasn't a hundred percent fit, so business wasn't done. Again we almost bought one back, this is British Football and judgment. We seemed to have a habit of letting players go who ended up at Oldham, one more was another boy I found at U-12, but not considered good enough at U-14 and released. His name is Andrew Holt. **Andrew Holt** is a tall left-sided defender, better than anything we had in his age group in defense at that time, in my estimation. He has gone on to have a successful career at Oldham and holds a regular place in their squad upto present date. These boys were all good honest lads and I was pleased for all of them, for not giving up after being rejected. They were determined to succeed no matter what.

I had a few that got away whilst I was at Leeds who went on to make the grade. There was **Jim Gordon** in 1971 a Goalkeeper who played for Stretford Boys and got 5 England Schoolboy caps he signed for Blackpool and later for Manchester United. **John Gannon** who in

1970 played for Manchester Boys also got 5 England Schoolboy caps and later signed for City. Then there was **Trevor Ross** in 1972 who played for Ashton-Under-Lyne Boys and got 8 England Schoolboy caps and later signed for Arsenal, I'd approached his father, but agreement had already been reached with Arsenal. **Paul Waddington** who played for Manchester Boys in 1975 got 4 England Schoolboy caps and eventually signed for Crystal Palace.

One, who didn't get away, was **Aiden Butterworth** who played for North Yorkshire in 1976 and England Schoolboys 3 times. He eventually signed for Leeds, albeit after I'd left to join City, we had him down at City but hesitancy on City's part in taking him on led to him joining Leeds where he made his debut in 1981. Aiden wanted to come to City, he liked it here. He wasn't one for the glory and adulation, he preferred to lodge, whilst at City, with a City supporter in Stretford and loved the simple home cooking and family life. A nice lad indeed.

There will always be those who get away from you for whatever reason. Some you lose to the 'bigger' clubs, some who decide to go on to other ventures.

I had seen a boy play in the Manchester Schoolboys trials for under-14/15. He was playing on the right wing. He looked very gifted, with good pace, good ball control and a good clean shot. I went to discuss the boy's Footballing future with his father, who was at that time, a member of the Pakistan Cricket Team, the Boys name was **Amjad Butt**. They lived near the North Manchester Hospital in Cheetham Hill and the boy attended Central Grammar School near Belle Vue, Manchester. His great pace enabled him to evade the tough 'tacklers'. After the trials he was selected to play For Manchester Boys and I had the good fortune to be able to sign him on Schoolboy Forms for City. About a week later, Manchester Boys had a mid-week game against Sheffield Boys at Bramhall Lane, Sheffield.

Amjad was to play on the right wing and Ken Barnes younger son, **Michael Barnes**, was to play on the Left wing. The two boys 'murdered' the opposition, no two boys could have played better and Manchester won convincingly, the boy's pace and skills were too much for the opposition.

At the end of the game the large crowd, who were, obviously, mostly Sheffield supporters, gave the two boys a standing ovation. The Scouts that were present to view likely prospects were informed that both boys were at Manchester City. I reported my opinions to Ken, that I thought we had 'Two Stars of The Future'. Unfortunately, nature played tricks on both boys as they were involved in the coaching sessions.

They both showed a lot of sparkle and promise, but in Amjad's case, he began to deteriorate in form as he found his physical responses were not progressing. He hated the physical contact when competing with the older and more physical type amongst the Youth players. His progress was 'nil', though encouraged by Steve and the rest of the staff, it was to no avail, he was regrettably, released. Amjad is now, I believe, a practising Physiotherapist with a Rugby League side, upto present date.

In Michael Barnes case, he was making great progress as an apprentice and making great strides in catching up with older brother Peter, who was just beginning to enjoy stardom with City. Then illness befell Michael, that was far reaching and this prevented him from attaining what I and all his family and friends had hoped for him. He would have, in my opinion, made an excellent 'pro'. He was a gifted, skilled and honest young man, he could play it with either foot and had good control and pace, he could also play as a left-winger, but was more adept in a mid-field role, perhaps a bit tougher than Peter. He was always a pleasure to watch and I will always hold him in very high regard.

You're not always successful in your quest for obtaining the best talent available, some you lose to the bigger clubs, and some you lose for reasons beyond your or their control. Which brings to mind the **Ryan Giggs** 'controversy'. Yes, we had him at City until just prior to his fourteenth birthday in 1988. He came to us from Deans Youth Club in Swinton at 9 years old. He'd been found playing for his local school, Grosvenor Road, by Dennis Schofield and brought in to play for Deans. He showed great potential from the start. He came at the same time as Richard Edgehill came to City and they both progressed steadily through the ranks. Ryan went on to play for Salford Boy's U-14 and U-15. He was training with us on a part time basis until just before his fourteenth birthday. We became very friendly with Ryan's father, who had been a prominent Rugby League player, but we neglected to establish a friendly relationship with his mother.

A domestic situation arose where Ryan's parents separated and Ryan went to live with his mother. Then enterprising Man United Scout's, found out that he wasn't signed to Schoolboy forms, and he was persuaded to exercise his freedom and, to sign for Manchester United. OK! Perhaps the situation of his parents separation may have been City's undoing, as Ryan chose domesticity with his Mother and adopted her maiden name Giggs, rather than Wilson, (His Fathers name) as we knew him. The United Scout's, knowing Ryan wasn't tied to a Schoolboy Form with City, watched his progress at Schoolboy level and, the rest is history.

I ask the question...

> "Would Ryan have blossomed and made the grade at City, and progressed to become the World Class player he is today, with little or no support to a fading Youth policy at Manchester City?"

All credit to the United Scout, who diligently inquired if he was committed to City! Finding he wasn't! Then taking the necessary action. A lesson learned. Or was it? Ryan wasn't the only one we lost to United that has gone on to achieve success.

Wesley Brown was with us at eleven-year old. I spotted Wes playing for Fletcher Moss Boy's Club, a great provider of Footballing talent, whilst watching a game with a colleague of mine, Wilf Ford. Wes was playing centre-half, and with some skill, I might add. Club Secretary, Ron Jamieson, gave us permission to invite Wes down to City for us to assess his capabilities. It's not often I miss attending trials when I have a prospect in, but I had to go to Belfast to work for a week. When I returned and inquired as to how he had done at the trial, Terry Farrell told me that he hadn't shown up and no invitations for a return visit were extended to him.

Two years later I was at a Manchester Schools game and I bumped into Wes' dad, and asked as to how Wes was getting on. I also asked as to what happened on the day he came for his trial at City. He was incensed at the lack of civility and reception they received upon their arrival. He also added that none of his kid's would ever attend a trial with City in the future. Another good prospect lost to a lack of interest in a fading Youth development. But again I ask the same question...

"Would Wes Brown have developed into the player he's become, with a fading Youth Development at Manchester City?"

There are the ones you've found, but because of poor judgment on the part of others, are let go and go on to prove, by their determination and self belief, that they have a career somewhere in this grand game of ours. One such boy that I sent along to City as an eleven year old, did just this. His name is Mark Mettrick.

Mark Mettrick is now 35 years old and has the honour of being head coach of the Maryland, U.S.A. State Team that will be touring Scotland in the summer of 1999. He came to City and played in our Junior side Whitehill, that Barry Bennall was in charge of at the time. Bennall was refused the post of Youth Development Officer at City and consequently took his Junior players with him to Crewe Alexandra where he obtained a post as assistant Youth Coach.

He told all the youngsters that he'd taken with him that they could have no more contact with City. Some did as he asked, others didn't. One of these was Mark. He continued to train at City, but was then told by City's new Youth Team Coach at that time, Tony Scott, that he wasn't considered good enough and he released him.

Mark continued to play with Whitehill Juniors, but again Crewe told him that there would be no Apprenticeship forthcoming. Mark was devastated, but not defeated. Mark went on to study at Loretto College at 16 years old and eventually made the Manchester County Schools Team at Under-19. He was playing alongside Paul McGuiness, who at this point in time, is Manchester Uniteds Youth Development Officer. He was then offered a part-time contract at United, where he played for about twelve months.

He was then spotted by a top US.A. College coach by the name of, Jeff Tipping. Mark was offered the opportunity of a combined Study and Playing Scholarship at Hartwick College in Oneouta, New York. In 1985/86 he was selected to play for the All American Colleges Team and then went on to play professional Football for the Baltimore Blast. He eventually turned to coaching where he became head coach of Mount St.Marys College, Maryland and finally Senior Coach to the Maryland State Side.

Apart from his State Coaching duties, he runs Summer Soccer Camps for some 1500 kids from all across America. I Illustrate Mark as my ideal of a lad, who had a belief and determination in himself, to succeed. Well done Mark, and may your success continue.

Although I had a few who got away, I take a lot of satisfaction in knowing that, somewhere along their way I had a helping hand in them having a career in football. This is what Scouting is all about. There are so many people in all walks of life and many different vocations, that never get the opportunity to succeed at a higher level, or at any level. There are probably thousands of talented Football playing youngsters that have been missed somewhere along the way over the years, but thanks to a football Scout, there are those, that have been spotted, and given that opportunity to fulfil their ambitions.

Football Scouts come from all walks of life. There are no special schools for Scouts, with no exams to sit and no special training. The majority of Scouts that I met in my early days worked on the shop floor in some factory or behind the counter in some shop. His training is his passion for the game and a keen eye for spotting that something special that sets apart the good player from the average player.

I made lots of friends and acquaintances in the Scouting profession in my early years. Even though we may have been in opposite camps we had a respect for each other and of each other's judgments. I would like to, if I may, tell you about a couple of them. One such Scout and friend was John Shore.

John was a colleague at work as well as being a Scout for West Brom. He was a character and had a great sense of humour. He suffered a little with his health, but never complained and got on with what he had to do without ever a moan and always with a sense of humour. Typical of his humour was an occasion whilst I was still at Leeds United. I heard that John had had a heart attack and was taken to Manchester Royal Infirmary. Word got round to all his friends, and to all his football friends, that he had been taken to Hospital. He was, obviously, in intensive care at first and then transferred to an open ward. Being such a character and likable person, he obviously attracted quite a few visitors.

On his first night of being allowed visitors I arrived to find four at his bedside and four waiting at the end of the ward and with more arriving. We played a sort of game of 'tag' to get to his bedside. The ward sister was getting a little wise as to what was going on and she gave him quite a lecture about how he needed to rest and not, to have so many friends visiting him all at one time. Even she had to laugh when he said...

"Friends! These are just my creditors, they're worried I'm going to drop dead before I've paid my debts! Just wait until my real friends arrive".

John has passed away now, I'm sad to say. There was nothing I enjoyed more, than having a couple of pints with John after watching a game.

Another character and friend in the Scouting fraternity was 'Big' Charlie Fletcher, who Scouted for Sheffield Wednesday. He was a giant of a man - six-foot plus and sixteen stone with a sense of humour to match. He also, was in poor health, but what a good job he did for Sheffield Wednesday. I think he knew every 'bloody' kid in Yorkshire and Derbyshire that could kick a ball and their age and all that was needed to know about them. His sense of humour is typified in a prank we played on a particular Scout from another club we wont mention. No one particularly liked this 'Scout' and always ignored him, if at all possible. You established a comradeship amongst Scouts whilst you're out there competing for the signatures of prospective talent. You learned to respect each other. Occasionally the odd 'rotten egg' would appear. This particular story explains what I mean.

Charlie and I were watching a schoolboy game just outside Sheffield one Saturday morning. Charlie, then got into a conversation with a parent of a lad that had caught his eye. He was writing down all the boys details - age / school attended etc.etc. - he then noticed this particular 'Scout' eves-dropping on what he was doing. Having then obtained all the information he needed, he then began to write in one of his spare note books, without the other 'Scout' knowing what he was writing, the correct name of the boy he was looking at, but about a fictitious game the boy would be playing in. He wrote down the directions as how to get there. The fictitious place was quite some distance away and not a Footballing venue.

Charlie then proceeded to put the notebook, with the false information into his pocket, but accidentally let it fall to the ground. Charlie and I then moved a little further down the pitch and discreetly watched the 'Scout' pick up the notebook with the phony information and pocket it.

The following week, at another schoolboy game. Charlie saw the 'Scout' and said to him...

"Did you enjoy you're visit to the Farm for the pig sale?".

The 'Scouts' response is unworthy of mentioning. The directions Charlie had written to the fictitious game, were at a Pig Farm that was quite some considerable distance away. Charlie proved a point, that there were a lot of dishonest people in the Scouting game also. I'm sad to say that Charlie has now passed away also. Another great loss to Football and to Sheffield Wednesday in particular, he was a great character.

Having friends like him makes your life so much richer. This was why I became a Scout in the early days. The friends and friendships made it worthwhile. It wasn't for the monetary riches, they just aren't available. My associates at AVROS (British Aerospace) thought I was 'barmy' to give up my time and a half for Saturday work and double time for Sunday, to go out in all weathers to watch a game of Football.

I placed a lot of emphasis on the friends, and friendships I made whislt fulfilling my duties. One friend I made early in my Scouting career was a most helpful friend, and one most of the Footballing World will always remember for his achievements on and off the field of play. We would often get together in Ken Barnes Office for a chat and a cup of coffee. They were very informal get togethers, more a laugh and joke than anything else, usually Ken, myself and any other member of staff who might be around.

Occasionally Ken would get a visit from fellow ex-professionals, now retired from playing, but who liked to keep in touch. One of these ex-players, the 'King' Dennis Law, would stop by, at least once a week. I'd never met Dennis as a player, but met him quite a lot at these informal chitchats. Dennis has a good sense of humour and is always ready for a bit of fun. He would often pose a question, usually a general knowledge question with the subject matter being on the English language proper, as spoken.

This was a subject at which Dennis is a master, having taken English and elocution lessons for years. Invariably Ken would provide an answer in his Midlands 'Brum' accent, at which Dennis would obviously refute as incorrect because of Ken's pronunciation. Ken would then come back with his own appropriate choice of 'four letter' language, at which we would all have a good laugh. Dennis was a good 'angler' and Ken always got 'hooked'. It was all in good fun though.

Dennis is a good speaker and is greatly admired by all that know him. He liked to discuss Football and any other subject you would care to choose. He could have made a fortune on the after dinner speaker circuit, but he declined the many offers. Just to say hello or pose for a photo with him, or his mere presence, would have sufficed his many admirers. I can recall one occasion when a friend of mine, Jeff Mellor, who was President of Ashton Boys Club who had arranged a Sports Presentation for a Friday evening in June. The youngsters, who were to be the recipients of the Trophies that were being handed out, were informed that a top Sporting personality would be making the presentations.

Jeff rang me on the Wednesday evening to say that Mike Doyle, the Manchester City Captain at that time, had had to withdraw because of some urgent business commitment.

Jeff was in bit of a fix and he asked me if I knew of someone who could step in at this short notice so as not to let the kids down. I took a chance and gave him Dennis Laws private phone number. Jeff rang Dennis. Dennis was very polite and asked Jeff who had given him his number. Jeff told him that it was me and told him the reason why, that Mike Doyle had had to let them down at the last minute because of an urgent matter. Dennis told Jeff, that although he had an engagement on that night near Sale, he would be happy to do the honours at 8.00pm, but must be away as soon as possible after 9.00pm.

Jeff offered to provide transportation to pick him up and take him back to where he was going. Dennis declined and just asked for directions. He promptly attended and did a tremendous job for a lot of happy Tameside boys and girls. When asked as to what his fee would be, he said nothing, just send me a boys club tie. He even came back on another occasion and did a repeat performance, because he said that he had enjoyed himself so much the first time. I don't see much of him these days, but it is a pleasure to be in his company whenever I do. To be able to enjoy the company of such a great man is a reward gained in conjunction with doing a Scouts job. I can honestly say that I made a lot of friends and gained a lot of respect as I went about my Scouting duties, and thats what made it all the more worthwhile. Having the respect of, and having respect for, such men as...

Dennis Law... This humorous and gifted Scotsman, has been slow not to capitalise on his second gift as a brilliant orator, with a command of English spoken better than most Englishmen.

George Taylor... My first mentor in the world of scouting. Footballs number one gentleman, the essence of respect.

Geoff Saunders... Ex-Grammar School Headmaster, and assistant Youth Officer at Leeds United. Commanded respect at any level, but taught many it's meaning.

Alan Hill... The Current Leeds United Youth Development Officer. Whilst at Manchester City, he was quiet and unassuming, but thorough and always respectful in my dealings with him.

Brian Kidd... Who has never lost his roots. A credit to his Manchester origins. Always has the respect of his associates, and will attain further laurels after his early management mishap.

Bob Shaw... Ex-Colleague for a short while at City. Went to Mansfield Town where he was mentor and advisor to Nickey Weaver. Bob's influence and persuasive powers enabled Jimmy Frizzell to bring Nickey to City, before Bob moved on to Chief Scout at Notts County. A shrewd but honest Yorkshire lad who does a great job, always respectful.

These are just a few whose associations made my associations, happy ones. Costing nothing but respect.

Len Davies – Terry Dunfield

"Terry Dunfield and Me at the Platt Lane Complex"

Leon Mike and Terry Dunfield

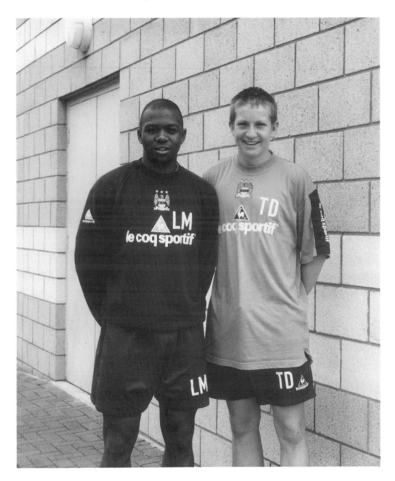

"Two for the future"

Chapter 8

"Footballs Responsibilities"

In reflecting back on almost fifty years, up to present date 2000, of playing, refereeing and a lifetime of Scouting in Football and of providing quite a few lads that have made it into the Pro-Ranks. I think I'm entitled to voice my opinion, and say, it is about time that we in Britain face up to the fact that, not much progress has been made in our coaching of the game.

The standards of coaches and coaching have fallen far below that of other Footballing nations in my estimation.   I believe that the Football Association and Professional Football in general, placed far too much emphasis on the Professional side of the game and on winning at that level.   In doing so, it neglected and disregarded, until the latter years, in constructing a good Youth policy including, Junior and Schoolboy soccer comparable to our European and the Third-World nations we tutored. Yes we taught them how to play the game, and we then sat back and stagnated until the late seventies or so.

Too much emphasis was placed on the professionals and after a drubbing or two did anyone take notice.   Our outdated teachings with little or no revisions were introduced. We then began to observe the Continental methods of coaching to enable us to perhaps develop better methods of training, but overlooking perhaps the necessary facilities and essentially the finances to implement the change.

My belief is that our kids were taught to soon to play 'positional' soccer. Whereas our Continental and Third World opponents were being taught the very sensible basics of - Footwork - Control - Passing -

Shooting - Heading and Possession, therefore enabling their youngsters to emerge as accomplished outfield players who are variant and adaptable to play in most positions.

We, I believe, had not studied, nor prepared our coaches to move with the times. I also believe that a unison of thought between the Football Association and Professional Footballers Association plus the Education Authorities of the U.K. (Which even todate are not excisting as an amiable working body) should produce an updated amalgamation of thoughts to progress our game to the highest level.

Even as I write - a true and co-operative level of liason between the F.A. and the Schools F.A. still does not exist fully in 2000.

We are, at last, I'm pleased to say, **slowly** beginning to progress to the stage we should be at, with the setting up of Football Academies plus Centres of Excellence for the coaching of Junior Footballers in the Major Cities and Towns. These are essential requirements, required by the Premier Division and more affluent Clubs. Whereby children, from the ages of seven and upwards, can begin the initial stages of their coaching skills as our neighbours on the Continent do. Playing in non-competitive games of 5/6/7 and 8-a-side until they progress to the age, where they are mature enough to compete at eleven a side.

This is a new structure that is finding it's way, but not readily accepted by all. We have the 'Them' v 'Us' friction. 'Them' of course, are the Schools and Junior Soccer in General. 'Us' are the F.A. and Professional Football.

Kids the World over want to play Football. They would play morning noon and night if we let them.

Common sense tells us this isn't possible. So disciplines and guidelines have to be introduced to control this. Common-sense controls that Mum-Dad-Grandad, the Teachers plus Local Football and those at the top, that are running the game, can all accept as a basis whereby, any youngster can enjoy a freedom to play for his School / Sunday Team and Pro-Club. Acceptable as long as, he or she conforms to a formula set up by a joint agreement between the Governing bodies - the F.A. - P.F.A. - Schools F.A. and County Associations on the amount of football they play.

Professional Football needs a continuous supply line of young Footballing talent in order to progress. Without it's continuous supply of young talent, Pro-Football would obviously stagnate. It stands to reason that Pro-Football wants to guard its 'Pupils', and safeguard their well-being. The need to restrict the number of games they play in order to preserve them for the rigors of their Footballing future. Some parents don't agree with this philosophy and feel that their 'offspring', if selected to play for his Town Team from the age of eleven upwards and even at a later date, being selected to play for England Schoolboys, should be allowed to do so. The boy may feel honoured to play and wish to do so personally.

This should be his prerogative and not denied him. The Pro-Clubs on the other hand feel that perhaps this is too much. Having to train 2/3 nights a week with them and then having to train with the Town or County Association and then playing on a Saturday and Sunday is too big a load for them to carry.

This is a problem that needs solving. It is the responsibility of Football to come up with an acceptable solution to all. Surely the F.A., the Schools F.A., and the County Associations are strong enough bodies to be able to come to an acceptable harmonious environment for all concerned. I believe they eventually will.

Scouting has turned a few corners since I first started in the 50's and now, finally, with the new guidelines that are being set up by the governing bodies in the recruitment of talented football playing schoolboys, the 'cloak and dagger' style of Scouting is disappearing. It is still around, but perhaps not as prevalent as it was in the early days. Now, because of these new guidelines being set up by the governing bodies, talented schoolboy players can now only be approached by following the correct procedure. Scouts must contact the Clubs they are registered with or through the schoolteacher in order to obtain permission to approach. These guidelines are there to protect both the player and the club from the 'cloak and dagger' approach. Occasionally it may breakdown for whatever reason, but on the whole it works.

The talented youngsters are now protected by contracts they sign with the Schools of Excellence, or the Football Academies, laying out their particular entitlements. Their welfare and education is now catered for also. The present day Scout now has to be a lot more aware of his responsibilities to the boys he is approaching and the Club he represents. He now has to be registered and participate on a 'Child Protection Awareness Course'. I mention this mainly because of the seriousness of what happened in 1998 in the Case of convicted Paedophile Barry Bennall. (* See Chapter .4.*)

Football in England will, I believe, eventually achieve its greatness once more in World Football domination. I'm sure it will finally come up with a formula and system of producing the best Footballing talent available. In order to achieve this, it will still need its regular supply of good 'home grown' youngsters. They will still be provided by the dedicated lovers of this beautiful game of ours - the Mum and Dad - the Postman - the Milkman - the Man who works at British Aero-Space and the Decrepit Old Man with the 'dodgy ticker'. Yes, the 'Football Scout' is really necessary.

I hope that you the reader have derived as much enjoyment from my scouting reminisces, as I have had in putting them together. My purpose fulfilled, if I gain recognition, not only for myself, but also for all my colleagues who, in the latter years, have chosen to try to attain some acknowledgment as scouts. I hope recognition with better financial rewards for their efforts, from Management and Directors alike. As Don Revie said...

"Give them all a slice of the cake".

A little thought on the part of the F.A. or the P.F.A. to have a look at Football Clubs Scouting Networks, to establish some basic parameters, for recognition of achievement on behalf of the scout. The Scouting movement is here, now, a necessary requirement, an essential part of any progressive minded club.

Summary

Now that it's all over and finished, I would like to emphasise once more, that this venture has been for my Lily (Mrs.Davies). Any other woman would have deserted ship long ago, she has been my best find todate and I couldn't have done it without her.

My thanks once more to the Nurses and Sisters at Tameside Hospital, who watched over me when I was at my lowest, Angels all of them.

My thanks again to yourself Peter, for all you have done, I can't repay you enough.

In all my years of Scouting, my health has been very good and I put it down to the great joy it's given me in being able to mix with the salt of the earth. Where in the World can you find, as you will in Footballs Stadiums, supporters comparable to the ones we have here in Manchester, or the 'Geordies and the Scousers', almost penniless in supporting their teams, their sense of humour is lovely to listen to, and it's free.

To my rivals in competing for the youngsters, good men like 'Big' Charlie Fletcher of Sheffield Wednesday and John Shore of West Brom, they were essentially comedians cum Scouts - no one could but like them. Both did a great job, God bless them. To Junior Footballs 'un-sung heroes', the Club Secretaries. All friends who go, for the most part, un-rewarded. A huge thank you to all of them. Men like Alan Millea Secretary of Tameside Schools for over thirty years. In South Manchester, Ron Jamieson Secretary of Fletcher Moss F.C. ably assisted by his wife Christine. In North Manchester,

Alan Bradbury Secretary of Droylsden Juniors, always helpful, patient and honest. At Manchester City Ron Evans, Scout, chaperone, collector-taxi driver, who gives many hours for the cause. Malcolm Abbott, coaching for Tameside Schools Football. Coaching and Scouting for Manchester City. A 100% honest man, always available and ready to assist. There aren't enough thanks bestowed on these people, for the contributions given. I will say it for all, 'Thank you very much gentlemen!'

To John Collins, Kit Man at Manchester City. John came here nearly forty years ago, though working full-time at his occupation as an electrician, he would spend all his time at City doing odd jobs and wet nursing the full time playing staff, no one wanted for anything, or any job went undone when he was around. John would cycle to Maine Road and home again no matter what the weather may have been, and he still does so even today. Nobody knows their way around a dressing room like John. He has seen them all come and go players and managers alike and he has earned their respect for all the assistance he has given to them over the years. John is one piece of Manchester City history that shouldn't go un-noticed. A one hundred percent 'True Blue'.

Another of Manchester City's un-sung heroes I must mention, is Rod Owen. Rod has been with City since 1993, he is a great organiser. During Terry Farrell's time in charge of Youth Development, Rod was offered the opportunity to coach, organise and look after our U-11 to U-14's. Although we didn't play many fixtures in those age groups at the time, Rod would organise all the games whenever we did. He would get the boys together and generally does everything required in getting a good job done and with a lot of success too. When Jim Cassell came in, he realised this and offered Rod the opportunity of carrying on with his organising skills. He is still with us and providing good support to our Academy Staff at present date.

To every young man who fancies a go at Scouting. You must love Football. You will never get rich, unless you are lucky, but thankfully, the modern progressive management's, including Manchester City, do give as good as most for a job well done. Always try to be honest and plan your programme meticulously. Always stand by your opinions. Thats what Scouting is all about, as Don Revie said to me after I did a mission for him...

"Don't change your opinion to curry favour, always stand by your word! It's your opinion, so give it!"

To all the staff at Maine Road and the Platt Lane Complex that does a tremendous job in keeping this great club ticking over, it doesn't go un-noticed.

Finally I want to say a little about things as they are currently at Manchester City. It is four years on since Jim Cassell became Director of our Youth Academy and with his staff - Barry Poynton, Alex Gibson, Paul Power, Frankie Bunn and the Academy Team Coaches they have re-established the Youth Development of Manchester City and what a tremendous job they are doing. The support and financial backing now given to our kids is once again earning them the respect of Football lovers around the Manchester area and it is all down to Jim Cassell and his hard working team. Our standards are as high as any other club in the Northwest and it now takes a real 'good-un' to become a Manchester City Junior.

How proud we Scouts are when we see the boys turn out to train or play, kitted out in the best attire. Nothing is too good thanks to current Chairman David Bernstein and the other Board Members for the tremendous job they are doing in providing the necessary support needed to maintain the progress of our Youth Development. To Ex-Chairman Francis Lee for his support, initially, in the setting up of our Soccer In The Community Program which led to the beginning of our present day Academy. Their faith will be repaid when they see our youngsters emerging to take a first team place in 2/3/4 or 5 years from now. And as a prelude to this, is the 1999 Under-14 Squad winning both the Foyle and Milk Cups in Ireland without conceding a goal in open play, another huge bonus for Jim Cassell and his hard working Academy Team. I take my cap off to them all, for it seemed four years ago, that we were nearly down and out.

Now myself, along with Eric Mullender the longest serving Scout of some twenty-seven years with City, and all our Scouting colleagues, at Manchester City. It is a great feeling to see a new era emerging thanks to a tremendous finale in the Play-Off Final at Wembley on May 30th 1999 putting this Club back on the road to a deserved success. It was nothing more than these magnificent supporters deserved, with promotion from the Second Division. Thanks to Joe Royale, and all the players and backroom staff who together, have performed magnificently to put the Icing on the Cake for these magnificent supporters, we're finally back in the Premier Division where this wonderful Club belongs.

The writing of this book, has been my objective and achievement. I've accomplished my 'goal' now, as I see myself winding down on my activities. The heart is willing, but the legs are weak. I've enjoyed every moment and I thank you all.

Respectfully

Len Davis

Acknowledgments

Alan B2all MBE...
Blackpool / Everton / Arsenal and England.

"I was involved with Len Davies quite a lot whilst at Manchester City. Whenever there was a Youth match, Len was always there and I enjoyed my talks with him about his thoughts on Youth Development and Youth Football in general. He, along with the hundreds of other Scouts around the country, are the lifeblood of all Football Clubs, constantly seeking to find a 'Gem' "...

Brian Kidd...
Manchester City / Manchester United

"Len is one of the most respected people in the Greater Manchester Area, not just for his ability to spot talent, but for his honesty and integrity, my best wishes to him"...

Earl Barratt...
Manchester City / Oldham / Aston Villa
Sheffield Wednesday & England

"My first introduction to Len Davies was when I was playing for Royton Youth Club Sunday League team way back in 1983. After one particular game he spoke to my then manager about me. If I remember rightly, my manager Alf Knowles, who has unfortunately passed away, told me that a Scout from Manchester City was going to be at the match. He didn't tell me beforehand for fear of putting me off my game. When I eventually met Len he asked me to come to City for trials. I couldn't believe it, this was my chance to start on the professional ladder.

After three days of trials I waited for what seemed an eternity for the letter from City hopefully confirming they would be taking me on. During this time I had trials for my hometown club Rochdale. They wanted to take me on straight away. No disrespect to Rochdale, but I had a chance of joining Manchester City one of the biggest clubs around. I wasn't sure as what to do, so I phoned Len and told him of my dilemma. Len said he would get things moving along from the City end. A short time later the letter arrived asking me to join the YTS ranks at Manchester City Football Club.

Thats just a little insight into how Len Davies helped me get a foot on the ladder of professional football. Without doubt, Len has changed my life by giving me the opportunity to play football as a career. Len must have seen that little something in me that he thought was enough for me to make it. To this end I am indebted to him. Len has found a few players over the years and I know they would be as grateful as I am to an unassuming dedicated Scout, who certainly made it possible for a young boy from Rochdale to play for a host of top clubs, to play at Wembley and also play for England. We have kept in touch over the years and I know he has been watching me and taking an interest in how I was doing. I thank you Len for having the confidence in me, a raw young kid, to become an established professional footballer".

Alan Millea...
Tameside Schools Football Association

"A small stocky man in a dark blue overcoat and flat cap, lately with the aid of a walking stick, has been for many years, a fixture on the touchlines of Tameside Association Football matches. He is quiet and misses nothing as he follows the game and perhaps the performance of a particular boy. He has always been my friend and a mug of hot coffee from his flask, has comforted me on countless cold winter mornings and frosty evenings all over Greater Manchester and the surrounding counties, as he watched boys at all levels from under-11 through to County standard at under-15 and under-16".

"Len Davis - Little Big Man from Hadfield - is a great friend whom I have known for many years, we probably played football against each other, he for the Belle Vue Legion and I for the Railway Pub in Levenshulme, he was a veteran and I was a sixteen year old with the World before me. Those were days in the late 40's when we used to play in front of crowds of 2000 on the Red Recreation Ground on Casson Street. There were some great old players then and it was a really good learning platform for youngsters like myself".

"This is a man I feel privileged to know, he is a friend and by todays standards, a real old fashioned gentleman.   Let me qualify that statement.
We are now living in a period when 'old fashioned' ways and values of conducting oneself in a gentlemanly way, with good manners, pleasantness and straightforward truthfulness in ones dealings with others, tended to be scoffed at.   I love the way he has kept that innate

keenness to do his job well; never once failing to show interest in the boys he has 'spotted' over the years. To have such a friend these days, is a joy".

"My first meeting with Len on the Association / Scouting footing was way back in the Revie days when he was Scouting for Leeds United. We had quite a few enjoyable Sunday outings to Temple Newsham to play against a Leeds United junior side. These were in the days of Ashton Boys, which later became the Tameside Association. These were the days when Schoolmasters treated Club Scouts with great suspicion, mainly because of the way they went about their job, but no one ever had that feeling with Len. Len always played it straight and you knew he would always go about things in the right way and never abuse your relationship. He has never let me down".

"I remember how delighted I was to learn that Len had played for Ashton Boys in the 1930's and delighted again when he accepted a life membership of Tameside Schools Football Association. The years have slipped by and in that time he has 'spotted' many boys for Manchester City. His finds locally, remind me of the day at Mellands during a County Under-15 Individual Schools match in which Audenshaw School were playing and Len asked me for permission to approach Geoff Lomax. Geoff went on to savour a brief flirtation with the big time in Manchester City's first team and of course, there was Paul Lake!"

"Len's approach has always been the same when on 'official business', but I would like to think, that he and I have another relationship based on a deep-seated mutual respect for what we have both tried to accomplish in our different jobs. To strive always to do our very best, in a fair professional way, with the well being of our boys in their conduct both on and off the field and the skill that goes with it as our overall objective".

"I know that recently you have not been too well, me 'owd' lad, but keep on coming to watch the boys play as long as you can. Be assured that you have done a great job in Tameside and your friendship with many people in the World of Schoolboy Soccer is well appreciated and always will be".

Ken Barnes...
Manchester City / Wrexham

"I had 20 wonderful years with Manchester City as Chief Scout on the Senior Side and working with the Youth Development. 20 great years, trying to sort out the 'Wheat from The Chaff'. I had a great team of Scouts and enjoyed every moment of working with them, especially you Len. There is no better judge of young talent than you. I have always said 'I don't discover them, I only rubber stamp them after you've brought them in upon leaving School'. My sincere thanks and best wishes to you".

Andy Thackerey...
Halifax Town F.C.

"I've played almost 500 Football League games over a fifteen year professional career, and my mind often drifts back to the day, when as a fourteen year old boy playing for Huddersfield Schools, Len Davies approached me and asked if I would like to have trials for Manchester

City. I was accepted, and was a part of the successful F.A. Youth Cup winning team in 1986. Hopefully, Mr.Davies's judgment has been justified over the years, and the enjoyment I have had, in being paid to do something I love day in and day out, can all be credited to Len Davies. To spot potential players at such an early age is a skill in itself. Hopefully, all the players Mr.Davies has recommended to Manchester City in particular, and who have gone on to play professional Football, will have given him so much enjoyment and pride over the years, as their careers have developed" .....

Kim and Sharon Dunfield...
Parents of Terry Dunfield - Manchester City F.C.

"Terry first met Len Davies during the summer of 1995. He had been competing with the British Columbia U-14 Team in a tournament (Keele Classic) in Crewe. A friend had asked Terry and another boy (Chad) if they would like to join up with Ted McDougall, who would already be over here with 3 older boys and go to 5 or 6 different clubs in England for the experience. As Terry was in love with his soccer and with the rest of the family looking forward to vacationing in England, this trip was arranged. The first club the boys went to was Manchester City where Alan Ball, a friend of Ted McDougalls was manager. The boys joined in with their age group from the club and from what we remember Len evaluated the boys ability. Manchester City made all of us feel very welcome and the boys remained here, although they did go to Liverpool for one day".

"We remember the day before we were to leave, Len came and talked to us about Terry. He said that

Terry had a good football mind and a good feel for the ball, but like anything, if he was to progress he should continue to practise and mentioned he should work with a smaller ball. He also gave us his card and told us he would like to stay in touch with Terry and follow how he was progressing. Also to let Terry know how the boys he had spent the last week with were getting on as well as first team and club news. For someone to offer this to a soccer crazy young thirteen year old boy was so kind even though we didn't know if anything would materialise. They corresponded back and forth, with the boys, Terry and his brother Ryan eagerly awaiting news from abroad. Since living in England, Len has continued his relationship with the family and we hope he sees us as family friends as well".

"We trust Len because of his honesty and also because of the wisdom he always passes on to Terry. Each letter Terry receives has a lesson, be it about work ethic or letting him know he has a long way to go and not be full of himself, etc. As parents we know Len will always tell us even if Terry does not reach the level required, which to us is as important or more to know. If you look at Len and you visualise what the perfect English Scout might be, it would be him. When we asked Terry what he thought of Len he said that he was very kind - words not very often expressed by a seventeen year old boy. In years to come Terry will think back to and hopefully re-read his letters, which we've kept and realise that he's been very lucky to have him in his life".

List of Photographs

INDEX

Page Number

Ellis, Sam:	76-77
Evans, Ron:	142
Farrar, David:	38
Farrell, Terry:	16-74-76-77-78-81-125-142
Felix, Gary:	2655
Fenlon, Billy:	23-24
Fenton, Anthony:	15
Fenton, Nick:	25-68
Fleet, Steve:	63-64-66-67-70-89-94-97-98-103
Fletcher, Charlie:	1-118-129-141
Flitcroft, Gary:	68
Foster, John:	68
Fox, Jimmy:	87
Frizzell, Jimmy:	27-76-79-82-83-120-133
Gannon, John:	121
Gemmill, Archie:	43
Gibson, Alex:	87-114-143
Giggs, Ryan:	12-124
Godwin, Harry:	63
Gordon, Jim:	121
Gray, Eddie:	49
Gregson, Bill:	49-50
Halford, Bernard:	71
Harrop, David:	40
Hart, Paul:	63
Harte, Ian:	18
Hatton, Richard:	31
Heaney, Paul:	53
Heaton, Paul:	119
Heighway, Steve:	50
Hill, Alan:	81-85-86-133
Hilton, Ronnie:	57
Hinchcliffe, Andy:	68
Hodgson, Steve:	19-68

MANCHESTER SPORTS

Everything for the football team under one roof.

We provide everything from Football Kits and Referee's Jerseys to Footballs and Stirrup Pumps. Distributors for Mitre, Prostar, Hummel, Adidas and more. We save team managers time AND money

We supply unbeatable quality at unbelievable prices.

Trophies, Drill Tops, Tracksuits, Sub Suits, Goalposts, and much more.

You can find us on the internet @ www.manchestersports.co.uk or you can contact our showroom to view any of the above range
Tel: 0161 366 1212 Fax: 0161 366 1177
Unit F2, Newton Business Pk, Talbot Road, Hyde, Cheshire. SK14 4UQ

Manchester Sports is proud to support Len Davies and we all wish Len all the best with his book.